John Mason Neale

The Moral Concordances of Saint Anthony of Padua

John Mason Neale

The Moral Concordances of Saint Anthony of Padua

ISBN/EAN: 9783337341220

Printed in Europe, USA, Canada, Australia, Japan

Cover: Foto ©Lupo / pixelio.de

More available books at **www.hansebooks.com**

THE
MORAL CONCORDANCES

OF

Saint Antony of Padua,

TRANSLATED, VERIFIED, AND ADAPTED TO
MODERN USE;

WITH SOME ADDITIONS FROM THE

PROMPTUARIUM MORALE OF THOMAS HIBERNICUS.

BY

THE REV. J. M. NEALE, D.D.,

WARDEN OF SACKVILLE COLLEGE.

Second  Edition.

LONDON: J. T. HAYES, LYALL PLACE, EATON SQUARE.
1867.

TO THE

REV. E. J. BOYCE, M.A.,

Rector of Houghton,

THESE CONCORDANCES ARE AFFECTIONATELY
DEDICATED.

INTRODUCTION.

1. If there were never a time when so many sermons issued from the press as at the present day, it is equally certain that, however much we may boast of our Scriptural knowledge, there never was a period when such compositions showed so little deep and ready acquaintance with the Bible. The actual quantity of reference to Scripture contained in the first volume of modern sermons which one may happen to take up, is surprisingly small: and further, the quotations are almost entirely made from favourite books—parade the same texts over and over again—leave vast portions of the Bible utterly untouched—and are superficially adduced without regard to their context. Now, whatever judgments may be formed in other respects of mediæval preachers, in this one thing it cannot be denied that they excel their successors. It is not merely that they quote ten texts for one in modern discourses; but that the passages they adduce are brought forward with impartiality, and according to analogy, from the Old and the New Testament; from the historical books and the prophets, as well, and as much, as from the Epistles and Gospels. This is what gives those sermons so much value. Their writers took, as it were, a bird's-eye view of the whole volume of Scripture

at once—saw, at a glance, what was most apposite—were as much at home in one portion as in another; and could, therefore, select the very text, or passage, which bore most strikingly on the point which they had in hand. Ours, on the contrary, wander up and down in some few trodden paths—never get out of them—never wish to look beyond them. Hence the fulness of the one, and the jejunity of the other, system.

2. S. Antony of Padua was not only one of the greatest, but, perhaps, the most popular, among the preachers of the Middle Ages. His extant Sermons, or, as they might rather be called, Sermon Notes, though coming down to us with all the disadvantages of their skeleton form, nevertheless evince a grasp of the Sacred Volume which well entitles him to the name bestowed on him by Gregory IX., —"*The Ark of the Testament.*" That which he exemplifies in his discourses, he shows in a not less striking manner by the "*Concordantiæ Morales,*" which are now, for the first time, presented to the English reader.

3. To enter into the question of the allegorical interpretation of Scripture in which the Middle Ages delighted, would require a volume instead of a preface.* It is not denied that many of the passages adduced by S. Antony could scarcely be quoted to a modern audience in the sense in which he applies them. Nevertheless even from these, by way of illustration, if not by way of proof, a

---

* Further remarks on this subject may be seen, if the reader wishes it, in the introduction to my *Mediæval Preachers.*

preacher of the present century might learn much, as a few examples, presently to be given will, perhaps, prove.

4. The "Moral Concordances" have come down to us in a very imperfect state. They were long supposed to be lost, and indeed considerable doubts were entertained whether such a book had ever existed. S. Antony died in 1231, and the manuscript was not discovered till about 1638, when it was disinterred in the library attached to the Church called Aracœli, in Rome. It seeems to have been published without very much attention to the correctness of its references; and as its author had, of course, merely referred to the chapter, without the verse, a great portion of the mistakes which occur may be owing to such (then necessary) vagueness of quotation. Further, it would seem that the subjects and the texts had been written in parallel columns, so that sometimes the verse which ought to have been last on one list, has found its way into the section which follows. The references are throughout most incorrectly given; one book even of Holy Scripture being sometimes substituted for another, while the chapters are very frequently wrong, and the verses in the later edition badly quoted in, perhaps, one instance out of three.

5. In the present edition all the references have been verified, and have been made to correspond with the authorised version—the Psalms, however, being quoted from the Prayer Book. The letter "f" refers to the former, "m" to the middle, and "l" to the latter part of a verse. It is possible that, in one or two cases, the

texts given are not those which S. Antony had quoted; it being very difficult, here and there, to decide whether there is a far-fetched allusion, or whether the transcriber has, by mistake, inserted a passage which has nothing to do with the subject.

6. The Concordances are said on the title-page to be adapted to modern use. The omissions are not at all of a doctrinal character, but simply falling under one or other of the following heads. (1.) Those which have no bearing on the duties of English Churchmen of the present day; such as—*Of the pride of Abbats, Of Pilgrimages, Of the Discipline of Monks,* and the like. In a book intended for use, it seemed worse than superfluous to swell the pages with references from which the modern Preacher could not possibly derive any advantage. (2.) Some sections are also omitted, based on half theological, half metaphysical divisions, which no one would now be able to introduce into any sermon. For instance: there are several headings, which are occupied with the various kinds of contemplation. "The first consists in imagination according to imagination; the second, in imagination according to reason; the third, in reason according to imagination; the fourth, in reason according to reason; the fifth is above reason, in a lower sense; the sixth is above reason, in a higher sense." It is clear that such a distribution of texts would now be of no practical use in the pulpit. (3.) When two sections, which is often the case, are occupied with subjects so nearly allied as to be almost identical, and when the

references given, are, for the most part, the same, then the second is very frequently omitted. (4.) In like manner, and also for the sake of brevity, references are very often omitted which have occurred in previous sections, in allusion to the same subject. (5.) In some instances, and more especially in the first book, sections referring to sins which could not possibly be treated of in the pulpit, have been left out; and the same may be said of minute subdivisions of other sins, such as, *The pride of the eyes, Of the neck, Of the arms, Of the shoulders, &c.* So that, in several cases, the last section only, generally thus summed up by S. Antony, *De precedentibus generaliter*, is the only one which is given. Perhaps this abbreviating process, so far as practical use is concerned, might have been advantageously carried somewhat further. (6.) In some cases a reference has necessarily been omitted, where, however beautiful the allusion to the words of the Vulgate, it would be utterly without sense when applied to our own version. Thus, the verse, *The* LORD *chose new wars*, is an excellent text for the festival of a virgin martyr, as setting forth the novelty of the conflict in which pain and death were overcome by a woman. But it would be useless to refer to the same text in our version; where we read, *They chose new gods; then was war in the gates.* So again, the grace of purity, as bestowed by the Holy Eucharist, is beautifully set forth by *Zech.* ix. 17, as it stands in the Vulgate;—" *For what is His goodness and what is His beauty, save the Corn of the Elect, and the Wine that blossoms into Virgins?*" The force of which is entirely lost by our English version: *Corn shall make the young men cheerful, and new wine the maids.* (7.) In several instances, and more especially at the beginning of the work, S. Antony has summed up the effects of a particular vice or virtue in a series of verses, not remarkable, generally speaking, either for their point or their terseness. In some cases, where the characteristics of one sin are nearly identical with those of another, they have been omitted; and in others, that which is verse in the Latin, has been put into prose. These are the principal alterations which have been made in the original book: and it has thus been reduced from 567 to 471 sections. It may be proper to observe, that nothing whatever has been added to the references selected by S. Antony.

8. We will give a few examples of the different ways in which the Moral Concordances might be useful in the present day. And first, of ingenious application of texts, which might well be used as illustrations. Separation from the world, if we would heartily serve God, is enforced by the example of Moses. (*Ex.* viii. 27.)—" We will go three days' journey into the wilderness, and sacrifice to the Lord our God, as He shall command us;" and, again, by the exhortation in the *Canticles*, iii. 11, (where the stress in this sense must be laid on the two first words,) " *Go forth*, O ye daughters of Zion, and behold King Solomon." The attacks to which we are exposed from the threefold temptations of the lust of the flesh, the lust of the eyes, and the pride of life, are illustrated by *Job* i. 17. " The Chaldeans made out

three bands;" by the threefold dangers of which Jeremiah speaks, (v. 6.)—" Wherefore a lion out of the forest shall slay them; and a wolf of the evenings shall spoil them; a leopard shall watch over their cities:" and by *Rev.* ix. 17—" Out of their mouths issued fire and smoke and brimstone; by these three was the third part of men killed; by the fire, and by the smoke, and by the brimstone." Against being assailed by violent temptation in the hour of death; (*S. Matt.* xxiv. 20)—" But pray ye that your flight be not in the winter." Against negligence in prayer: (*Jer.* xlviii. 10)—" Cursed be he that doeth the work of the LORD deceitfully." That a prelate should be diligent in his labours; (*Gen.* xlvii. 6)—" And if thou knowest any men of activity among them, then make them rulers over my cattle;" and *Prov.* xxvii. 23—" Be thou diligent to know the state of thy flocks, and look well to thy herds." Against pluralities; (*Exod.* xviii. 18) —" This thing is too heavy for thee; thou art not able to perform it thyself alone." And *S. Luke* xix. 21—" Thou art an austere man: thou takest up that thou layedest not down, and reapest that thou didst not sow." That ecclesiastical revenues are not to be laid out on the possessor's family; (*Lev.* xxii. 12) — " If the priest's daughter also be married unto a stranger, she may not eat of an offering of the holy things:" and *Prov.* xxviii. 24—" Whoso robbeth his father or his mother,"—that is—GOD or the Church—"and saith, It is no transgression; the same is a companion of the destroyer." That GOD sometimes chooses the greatest sinners to be

His most eminent servants; (*Prov.* xxxi. 14)—" She bringeth her food from afar." That preachers must not contradict their doctrines by their lives; (*Ps.* lxxxviii. 11) —" Shall Thy loving kindness be showed in the grave, or Thy faithfulness in destruction?" That preaching must be according to the capacity of the hearer; (*Gen.* xliv. 1) —" Fill the men's sacks with food, as much as they can carry." Against those who are negligent in preaching; (*Gen.* xxix. 10)—" Jacob went near, and rolled the stone from the well's mouth, and watered the flock:" and *Prov.* xi. 26—" He that withholdeth corn, the people shall curse him;" and xxii. 9—" He that hath a bountiful eye shall be blessed; for he giveth of his bread to the poor." Of the Passion of our LORD; (*Josh.* viii. 26)— " For Joshua drew not his hand back wherewith he stretched out the spear, until he had utterly destroyed all the inhabitants of Ai." Of the Last Judgment; (*Rev.* xvi. 19)—" Great Babylon came in remembrance before GOD, to give unto her the cup of the wine of the fierceness of His wrath." Of the Resurrection; (*Gen.* viii. 21)—" I will not again curse the ground any more for man's sake;" and *Cant.* i. 4—" Draw me, we will run after Thee;" as showing that our own resurrection is dependent on that of our LORD; and *S. John* xii. 32—" And I, if I be lifted up from the earth, will draw all men unto Me." For the Festival of S. Peter; (2 *Sam.* xv. 21)—" Surely, in what place my LORD the King shall be, whether in death or life, even there also will Thy servant be." (Compare *S. John* xiii. 37—" LORD, why cannot I follow Thee now?" I will lay down my life for Thy sake.") Of our LORD's Manifestation of His love in His Passion; (*Gal.* vi. 11)—"Ye see how large a letter I have written unto you with Mine own hand." For the Festival of an Apostle; (*Gen.* xlii. 13)—"Thy servants are twelve brethren, *the sons of one man in the land of Canaan.*" For the Festival of Martyrs; (*Nah.* ii. 3)—"The shield of His mighty men is made red: the valiant men are in scarlet." For the Festival of a virgin Martyr: (*Cant.* iv. 8)—"Come with me from Lebanon, my spouse, with me from Lebanon . . . . from the lions' dens, from the mountains of the leopards." For the Festival of Confessors: (1 *Kings* xii. 20)—"There was none that followed the house of David, but the tribe of Judah only."

9. As an example of the more obvious application of Scriptural texts and histories, take the following section, 138 in the original;

Against those that agree in evil; or that make a conspiracy against others.

Gen. xiv. 1. And it came to pass in the days of Amraphel king of Shinar, Arioch king of Ellasar, Chedorlaomer king of Elam, and Tidal king of nations, that . . . all these were joined together.

xxxiv. 25. Simeon and Levi, Dinah's brethren, took each man his sword, and came upon the city.

xxxvii. 18. Before he came near unto them, they conspired against him to slay him.

Ex. xxxii. 3. And all the people brake off the golden earrings which were in their ears, and brought them unto Aaron.

Num. xvi. 1. Now Korah, the son of Izhar, and Dathan and Abiram, the sons of Eliab, and On, the son of Peleth, took men: and they rose up before Moses, with certain of the children of Israel, two hundred and fifty princes of the assembly.

2 *Sam.* xv. 12. And the conspiracy was strong, for the people increased continually with Absalom.

Prov. i. 10. My son, if sinners entice thee, consent thou not.

Is. i. 23. Thy princes are rebellious, and companions of thieves.

viii. 12. Say ye not, A confederacy, to all them to whom this people shall say, A confederacy; neither fear ye their fear, nor be afraid.

Jer. xi. 9. And the LORD said unto me, A conspiracy is found among the men of Judah, and among the inhabitants of Jerusalem.

Jer. xxxviii. 5. Behold he is in your hand; for the king is not he that can do anything against you.

Dan. vi. 4. Then the presidents and princes sought to find occasion against Daniel.

Wis. ii. 10. Let us oppress the poor righteous man; let us not spare the widow, nor reverence the ancient grey hairs of the aged.

S. John xi. 47. Then gathered the chief priests and the Pharisees a council, and said, What do we?

Gal. v. 20. Seditions, heresies.

Here is another example, section 456 in the original;

That the righteous are ridiculed, and suffer persecution in the present life.

Gen. iv. 8. Cain rose up against Abel his brother, and slew him.
   xv. 13. Know of a surety, that thy seed shall be a stranger in a land that is not theirs, and shall serve them: and they shall afflict them four hundred years.
   xvi. 4. Her mistress was despised in her eyes.
   xix. 9. This one fellow came in to sojourn, and he will needs be a judge; now will we deal worse with thee than with them.
   xxi. 9. And Sarah saw the son of Hagar the Egyptian, which she had born unto Abraham, mocking.
   xxvi. 14. And the Philistines envied him.
   xxvii. 41. And Esau hated Jacob because of the blessing wherewith his father blessed him.
   xxxi. 23. And he took his brethren with him, and pursued after him seven days' journey.
   xxxvii. 4. And when his brethren saw that their father loved him more than all his brethren, they hated him, and could not speak peaceably unto him.
Ex. i. 12. And they were grieved because of the children of Israel.
Num. xvi. 3. Ye take too much upon you, seeing all the congregation are holy, every one of them.

1 *Sam.* xxi. 14. Lo, ye see the man is mad; wherefore then have ye brought him to me?

xxiii. 14. And Saul sought him every day, but God delivered him not into his hand.

2 *Sam.* xvi. 7. Come out, come out, thou bloody man, and thou man of Belial.

2 *Chron.* xxx. 10. So the posts passed from city to city . . . but they laughed them to scorn.

Job ii. 9. Dost thou still retain thy integrity? curse God, and die.

xii. 4. The just upright man is laughed to scorn.

xix. 18. Yea, young children despised me; I arose, and they spake against me.

xxx. 1. But now they that are younger than I have me in derision.

9. And now am I their song, yea, I am their byword.

Ps. ii. 2. The kings of the earth stand up, and the rulers take counsel together.

iii. 2. Many one there be that say of my soul: There is no help for him in his God.

xxii. 12. Many oxen are come about me: fat bulls of Basan close me in on every side.

lxix. 11. I put on sackcloth also: and they jested upon me.

lxxxiii. 2. For lo, thine enemies make a murmuring; and they that hate thee have lift up their head.

cix. 4. Thus have they rewarded me evil for good: and hatred for my good will.

Prov. xiv. 2. He that walketh in his uprightness feareth the Lord; but he that is perverse in his ways despiseth him.

xix. 28. An ungodly witness scorneth judgment.

xxix. 10. The bloodthirsty hate the upright.

27. He that is upright in the way is abomination to the wicked.

Is. xxxvi. 4. And Rabshakeh said unto them, Say ye now to Hezekiah, Thus saith the great king, the king of Assyria, What confidence is this wherein thou trustest?

liii. 2. He hath no form nor comeliness; and when we shall see Him, there is no beauty that we should desire Him.

Jer. xvii. 15. Behold they say unto me, Where is the Word of the LORD? let it come now.

xx. 8. The Word of the LORD was made a reproach unto me, and a derision, daily.

Lam. ii. 16. All thine enemies have opened their mouth against thee: they hiss and gnash the teeth, they say, We have swallowed her up: certainly this is the day that we looked for; we have found, we have seen it.

iii. 14. I was a derision to all my people; and their song all the day.

Wis. v. 3. This was he, whom we had sometime in derision, and a proverb of reproach.

S. Matt. xxvii. 29. And they bowed the knee before Him, and mocked Him, saying, Hail, King of the Jews!

S. Luke xxiii. 11. And Herod with his men of war set Him at nought, and mocked Him.

S. John viii. 48. Say we not well that Thou art a Samaritan, and hast a devil?

xv. 19.   Because ye are not of the world, but I have chosen you out of the world, therefore the world hateth you.

Acts xxvi. 24. Paul, thou art beside thyself; much learning doth make thee mad.

1 *Cor.* iv. 9.   For we are made a spectacle unto the world, and to angels, and to men.

S. James ii. 6. But ye have despised the poor.

10. We will next take a section in which the meaning is more recondite; and the references such as would now probably be used rather by way of illustration than of proof. It is in the original 472 :—

> *That the memory of the* LORD's *Passion gives comfort, and sweetens all evils.*

Ex. xii. 13. And when I see the blood, I will pass over you; and the plague shall not be upon you to destroy you.

xv. 25. The LORD showed him a tree, which when he had cast into the waters, the waters were made sweet.

xxviii. 38. And it shall be upon Aaron's forehead, that Aaron may bear the iniquity of the holy things . . . . and it shall be always upon his forehead, that they may be accepted before the LORD.—[This golden plate is interpreted by mediæval writers of our LORD Himself: by Whom, according to this explanation, all Christians, as a royal priesthood, receive pardon of their sins, and acceptance with GOD.]

Num. xx. 11. And with his rod he smote the rock twice, and the water came out abundantly.

xxi. 8. Make thee a fiery serpent, and set it upon a pole: and it shall come to pass, that every one that is bitten when he looketh upon it, shall live.

Josh. ii. 21. She bound the scarlet line in the window.

1 *Sam.* ii. 16. Let them not fail to burn the fat presently, [or, as it is in the Vulgate, *first*], and then take as much as thy soul desireth; [that is, by means of the Passion of CHRIST first suffered, all that the soul of His people can desire, is given to them: a parallel passage in this sense, with " He that spared not His Own SON, but delivered Him up for us all, how shall He not with Him also freely give us all things?"]

1 *Kings* xvii. 3. Get thee hence, and turn thee eastward, and hide thyself by the brook Cherith, that is before Jordan.

2 *Kings* iv. 40. O thou man of GOD, there is death in the pot. But he said, Then bring meal, and he cast it into the pot . . . . and there was no harm in the pot. [That is, the wild gourds are a type of sin; the vessel, of the human heart; the meal, of the Holy Eucharist, and its effect in preserving against the dangers of temptation.]

Ps. xxv. 20. Let perfectness and righteous dealing wait upon me. [That is, the perfect righteousness of our LORD: *wait upon me*, in the sense of that verse, " The SON of MAN came not to be ministered unto but to minister."]

Ps. civ. 18. So are the stony rocks for the conies. ["That rock was CHRIST."]

Prov. iii. 18. She is a tree of life to them that lay hold upon her; and happy is every one that retaineth her.

xxx. 26. The conies are but a feeble folk, yet make they their houses in the rocks.

Eccles. ix. 14. Now there was found in it a poor wise man, and he by his wisdom delivered the city; yet no man remembered that same poor man.

Cant. i. 13. A bundle of myrrh is my Well-Beloved unto me; he shall lie all night betwixt my breasts.

ii. 2. I sat under His shadow with great delight, and His fruit was sweet to my taste.

14. O My dove, that art in the clefts of the rock.

viii. 6. Set me as a seal upon Thine heart, as a seal upon Thine arm.

Is. ii. 10. Enter into the Rock.

Ezek. ix. 6. Slay utterly old and young, both maids, and little children, and women: but come not near any man upon whom is the mark.

Ecclus. xiv. 25. He shall lodge in a lodging where good things are.

xxix. 17. He that is of an unthankful mind will leave Him that delivered him.

xxxviii. 4. The LORD hath created medicines out of the earth, and he that is wise will not abhor them.

1 *Macc.* vi. 34. And to the end they might provoke the elephants to fight, they showed them the blood of grapes and mulberries.

Heb. xii. 3. For consider Him that endured such contradiction of sinners against Himself, lest ye be wearied and faint in your minds.

Take as another example, section 466 :—

Of the Incarnation and Nativity of CHRIST.

Gen. xlix. 10. The sceptre shall not depart from Judah, nor a lawgiver from between his feet, until SHILOH come; and unto Him shall the gathering of the people be.

Ex. iv. 13. O my Lord, send, I pray Thee, by the hand of Him Whom Thou wilt send.

xxxi. 2. See, I have called by name Bezaleel the son of Uri, the son of Hur, of the tribe of Judah.

Num. xvii. 2. Speak unto the children of Israel, and take every one of them a rod according to the house of their fathers, of all their princes according to the house of their fathers twelve rods; write thou every man's name upon his rod, etc.

xxiv. 17. There shall come a Star out of Jacob, and a Sceptre shall arise out of Israel, and shall smite the corners of Moab, and destroy all the children of Sheth.

Deut. xviii. 15. The LORD thy GOD will raise up unto thee a Prophet from the midst of thee, of thy brethren like unto me; unto Him ye shall hearken.

Judg. vi. 37. Behold, I will put a fleece of wool in the floor; and if the dew be on the fleece only, and it be dry upon all the earth beside, then shall I know that Thou wilt save Israel by mine hand, as Thou hast said.

xiii. 2. And there was a certain man of Zorah, whose name was Manoah, and his wife was barren, and bare not, etc.

1 *Kings* viii. 12. The LORD said that He would dwell in the thick darkness: (the allusion is to the mystery of the Incarnation.)

Job xxxi. 35. Oh that one would hear me! Behold, my desire is, that the ALMIGHTY would answer me, and that mine adversary had written a book.

xxxiii. 23. If there be a Messenger with him, an Interpreter, one among a thousand, to show unto man his uprightness.

xxxviii. 6. Whereupon are the foundations thereof fastened? or Who laid the corner stone thereof?

Ps. ii. 7. I will preach the law, whereof the LORD hath said unto me: Thou art My SON, this day have I begotten Thee.

lxxii. 6. He shall come down like the rain into a fleece of wool: even as the drops that water the earth.

lxxvii. 14. Thou art the GOD That doeth wonders: and hast declared Thy power among the people.

lxxx. 1. Show Thyself also, Thou That sittest upon the cherubims,

cx. 1. The LORD said unto my Lord: Sit Thou on My right Hand, until I make Thine enemies Thy footstool.

cxliv. 5. Bow Thy heavens, O LORD, and come down: touch the mountains, and they shall smoke.

Prov. xxx. 4. Who hath ascended up into heaven, or descended?

xxxi. 10. Who can find a virtuous woman? for her price is far above rubies.

Eccles. vii. 28. One Man among a thousand have I found: but a woman among all those have I not found.

Cant. iii. 11. Go forth, O ye daughters of Sion, and behold King Solomon with the crown wherewith His Mother crowned Him in the day of His Espousals, and in the day of the gladness of His heart.

Is. i. 9. Except the Lord of Hosts had left unto us a very small remnant, we should have been as Sodom, and we should have been like unto Gomorrah.

ii. 2. And it shall come to pass in the last days, that the mountain of the Lord's House shall be established in the top of the mountains, and shall be exalted above the hills, and all nations shall flow unto it.

iv. 1. And in that day seven women shall take hold of one Man.

vii. 14. Behold, a Virgin shall conceive, and bear a Son, and shall call his name Emmanuel.

viii. 1. Take thee a great roll, and write in it with a man's pen concerning Maher-shalal-hash-baz.

ix. 6. For unto us a Child is born; unto us a Son is given.

xi. 1. And there shall come forth a Rod out of the stem of Jesse and a Branch shall grow out of his roots.

xvi. 1. Send ye the Lamb to the ruler of the land from Sela to the wilderness.

xix. 1. Behold, the Lord rideth upon a swift cloud, and shall come into Egypt.

xxviii. 16. Behold, I lay in Sion for a foundation a Stone, a tried Stone, a precious Corner-stone, a sure Foundation.

xxxv. 4. He will come and save you.

xl. 9. Say unto the cities of Judah, Behold your God.

Is. xlii. 1. Behold My servant Whom I uphold; Mine Elect, in Whom my soul delighteth.

xlvi. 11. Calling a ravenous bird from the east, the Man that executeth My counsel from a far country.

xlix. 1. The Lord hath called Me from the womb; from the bowels of My Mother hath He made mention of My Name.

lii. 13. Behold, My servant shall deal prudently; He shall be exalted and extolled, and be very high.

liii. 8. Who shall declare His generation?

liv. 1. Sing, O barren, thou that didst not bear.

lv. 4. Behold, I have given Him for a Witness to the people; a Leader and Commander to the people.

lx. 1. Arise, shine: for thy light is come, and the glory of the Lord hath risen upon thee.

lxi. 1. The Spirit of the Lord God is upon Me, &c.

lxii. 1. For Sion's sake will I not hold my peace, and for Jerusalem's sake I will not rest, until the righteousness thereof go forth as brightness, and the salvation thereof as a lamp that burneth.

lxiv. 1. O that Thou wouldest rend the heavens, that Thou wouldest come down, that the mountains might flow down at Thy presence.

lxv. 1. I said, Behold Me, behold Me, unto a nation that was not called by My Name.

lxvi. 7. Before she travailed, she brought forth; before her pain came, she was delivered of a Man Child.

Jer. xiv. 8. O the Hope of Israel, the Saviour thereof in time of trouble, why shouldest Thou be as a stranger in the land?

xv. 10. Woe is me, My Mother, that thou hast borne me a Man of strife and a Man of contention to the whole earth!

xxiii. 5. Behold, the days come, saith the Lord, that I will raise unto David a righteous Branch, and a King shall reign and prosper.

xxxi. 22. The Lord hath created a new thing in the earth: a woman shall compass a Man.

Ezek. xxxiv. 23. And I will set up one Shepherd over them, and He shall feed them, even My servant David.

29. And I will raise up for them a Plant of renown, and they shall no more be consumed with hunger in the land.

Dan. ii. 44. And in the days of these kings shall the God of Heaven set up a kingdom, which shall never be destroyed.

Dan. iii. 25. Lo, I see four men loose, walking in the midst of the fire, and they have no hurt; and the form of the fourth is like the Son of God.

vii. 13. I saw in the night visions, and, behold, one like the Son of Man came with the clouds of heaven.

ix. 24. Seventy weeks are determined upon thy people and upon thy holy city, to finish the transgression . . . and to anoint the Most Holy.

Hos. i. 11. Then shall the children of Judah and the children of Israel be gathered together, and appoint themselves One Head.

ii. 19. And I will betroth thee unto Me for ever; yea, I will betroth thee unto Me in righteousness.

vi. 1. Come, and let us return unto the Lord: for He hath torn, and He will heal us; He hath smitten, and He will bind us up.

xi. 1. When Israel was a child, then I loved Him, and called My Son out of Egypt.

xiii. 14. I will ransom them from the power of the grave: I will redeem them from death.

xiv. 5. I will be as the dew unto Israel.

Joel ii. 23. Be glad then, ye children of Sion, and rejoice in the Lord your God; for He hath given you the former rain moderately; and he will cause to come down for you the rain, the former rain, and the latter rain of the first month. And the floors shall be full of wheat.

Amos iv. 12. Prepare to meet thy God, O Israel.

Jon. i. 2. Arise, go to Nineveh, that great city, and cry against it.

Mic. i. 3. For behold, the LORD cometh forth out of His place, and will come down, and tread upon the high places of the earth.

15. Yet will I bring an Heir unto thee, O inhabitant of Mareshah.

v. 2. But thou, Bethlehem-Ephratah, though thou be little among the thousands of Judah, yet out of thee shall He come forth unto Me That is to be Ruler in Israel; Whose goings forth have been from of old, from everlasting.

Hab. ii. 2. Write the vision, and make it plain upon tables, that he may run that readeth it.

Hag. ii. 6. Yet once, it is a little while, and I will shake the heavens, and the earth, and the sea, and the dry land.

Zech. ii. 10. Sing and rejoice, O daughter of Sion; for, lo, I come, and I will dwell in the midst of thee, saith the LORD.

iii. 3. Now Joshua was clothed with filthy garments. (The allusion is, to the assumption by our LORD JESUS —the same name as Joshua—of the garment of our nature.)

8. Behold, I will bring forth My servant, the Branch.

viii. 23. In those days it shall come to pass, that ten men shall take hold out of all languages of the nations, even shall take hold of the skirt of Him That is a Jew.

Zech. ix. 9. Rejoice greatly, O daughter of Sion; shout, O daughter of Jerusalem; behold, thy King cometh unto thee.

xiii. 1. In that day there shall be a fountain opened to the house of David and to the inhabitants of Jerusalem, for sin and for uncleanness.

Mal. iii. 1. The LORD, Whom ye seek, shall suddenly come to His temple.

iv. 2. But unto you that fear My Name shall the Sun of Righteousness arise with healing in His wings.

Wis. xviii. 14. For while all things were in quiet silence, and that night was in the midst of her swift course, Thine Almighty Word leaped down from heaven out of Thy royal throne.

Ecclus. xxxviii. 4. The LORD hath created medicines out of the earth.

Bar. iii. 37. Afterward did He show Himself upon earth, and conversed with men.

1 *Macc.* xiv. 41. Also that the Jews and priests were well pleased that Simon should be their Governor and High Priest for ever . . . . moreover, that He should be their Captain, and should take charge of the sanctuary . . . . . beside this, that He should be obeyed of every man.

S. Matt. iii. 17. This is My beloved Son, in Whom I am well pleased.

S. Luke i. 30. Fear not, Mary; for thou hast found favour with GOD.

11. It cannot be denied that some of the references are so extremely far-fetched or allegorical, as to be utterly inapplicable to modern audiences, who have to learn, for the most part, the general principle of any symbolical teaching in Holy Scripture. Thus, that the soul of the proud man is the abode of Satan is proved by the text, referring to Behemoth;—"He lieth under the tall trees." That we ought frequently to call to mind our sins in order to confess them the more exactly, is taught from the three following passages. *Gen.* i. 9. "And God said, Let the waters under the heaven be gathered together unto one place, and let the dry land appear; and it was so." *Gen.* xxvii. 9. "Go now to the flock, and fetch me from thence two good kids of the goats; and I will make them savoury meat for thy father, such as he loveth." xxxviii. 17. "And he said, I will send thee a kid from the flock. And she said, Wilt thou give me a pledge, till thou send it?" The great truth, that a man is never so likely to be exposed to temptation, as when he has just received some especial grace, is taught from *Tobit* vi. 2; it was when Tobias had just been washing himself in the river that the fish leaped out upon him, and would have devoured him. Against the discrepancy between the lives and doctrine of wicked preachers. *Ps.* civ. 8. "They go up as high as the hills, and down to the valleys beneath." That the labourer is worthy of his hire. *Ps.* cxlvii. 8. "Who maketh the grass to grow upon the mountains;" the mountains being the emblem of preachers, and grass of their means of support. Of the Resurrection: *Eccles.* xii. 4—"He

shall rise up at the voice of the bird "—that is, of the Archangel. For the Festival of S. Andrew: 2 *Kings* iv. 32. " Behold, the child was dead, and laid upon his bed ; "— an allusion to S. Andrew's having suffered by being laid upon our LORD's bed—namely the Cross. For the Conversion of S. Paul: *Ecclus.* viii. 1—" Strive not with a mighty man, lest thou fall into his hands ; " the reference being to our LORD's Words, " Why persecutest thou Me ?"

12. It would have been my wish to adopt the same form as that of the original, and to print at length the first line of each text to which reference was made. But the size to which this would have swelled the present volume, making it an octavo of about 800 pages, rendered the arrangement impossible. One advantage will be found in the translation, the absence of which is a great drawback to the practical utility of the original, I mean the index. S. Antony's arrangement, although it be called by his editor "most excellent, and disposed in a most learned order," is rather confusing ; and one does not see any possible connection between succeeding sections in the same chapter. The account which is prefixed to the work, and which explains the contents of its five books, is as follows :—" The first book treats of those things which pertain to the fall and their opposites, divided into Four parts. The first, of sin in general, and its effects. The second, of the principal vices, and their contraries. The third, of sins of the tongue. The fourth of the preceding, taken together. The Second Book treats of those things which pertain to GOD, with

their opposites, and has two parts. The first, of endeavouring after the conversion of a sinner, and of the newly converted. The second is of the manner of conversion, which principally consists in contrition, in confession, and in satisfaction. The Third Book treats of those things which pertain to him that fights valiantly, or that is overthrown in the spiritual war ; and has two parts. The first contains the temptations of the devil, persecutions of various kinds, the use of tribulation, the Divine help, perseverance in good, and the Crown of eternal life, which is due to a good soldier of CHRIST. The second treats of inconstancy, backsliding, perseverance in evil, good and evil companions, and the eternal punishment which is due to him that is overthrown in the spiritual war. The Fourth Book treats of those things which pertain to a perfect man; and has four parts. The first is of the cardinal virtues. The second is of the theological virtues. The third of the active, the fourth of the contemplative, life. The Fifth Book treats of relative duties, and certain other matters ; and contains eight parts. The first is of prelates and priests, and their flocks. The second, of preachers, and those whose duty it is to rebuke. The third, of masters and servants. The fourth, of judges, lawyers, and oppressors of the poor. The fifth, of parents and children. The sixth, of the Unity and Trinity of GOD, and of CHRIST and Anti-christ. The seventh has the "Extravagant Rubrics;" (that is, the miscellaneous sections, for which no more appropriate position could be found.) The eighth treats of the Saints, in the order of the Calendar.

In this last section, I have, for brevity's sake, omitted those which are not contained in our own calendar; they are not, however, many.

13. In conclusion, the translator is only repaying a debt due to the labours of S. Antony, if he expresses the greater insight into Holy Scripture which the translation of the present work has given him. If others should derive but a quarter of the benefit that he himself is conscious of having gained from the Moral Concordances, that translation will not have been undertaken in vain.

SACKVILLE COLLEGE,
May, 1856.

PREFACE TO SECOND EDITION.

In this edition some additions have been made from the *Promptuarium Morale Sacræ Scripturæ* of Thomas Hibernicus, an Irish Franciscan who flourished at the beginning of the Fourteenth Century. It was first published, like the Concordances of S. Antony by Luke Wadding, at Rome, in 1624; he was, however, ignorant of the name of the author. Thomas was a man of some note in his day; and another valuable little work of his has been published, the *Deliciæ Sanctorum*: choice passages on various subjects, from the Fathers and later writers.

The *Promptuarium* is of the same nature as the Concordances; it is, however, nearly twice as long. The division is entirely different, consisting of three parts. The first goes through the regular course of Sunday and Feria; the second embraces the Festivals of Saints; the third supplies texts for Sermons to be addressed—almost literally—to all sorts and conditions of men. Some of the subjects in this last part are exceedingly curious.

It is plain that only in the second part do he and S. Antony touch the same matter; and my additions, distinguished by Italics, are therefore only made from that. The first part would be well worth republishing.

I had not ventured to hope that the Concordances would ever reach a second edition. I can only be thankful that the style of interpretation which they presuppose must thus have become better known to many of my brethren.

As a proof how large a field of mystical interpretation still remains, after these writers, to be gleaned, I will put down at random a few texts which have in the past year occurred to myself and to friends, as thus bearing a beautiful meaning:—

Christmas or Annunciation. 1 Sam. xxiii. 20 :—Now therefore, O King, come down according to all the desire of Thy soul to come down.

Holy Trinity. Is. ix. 4 :—For thou hast broken the yoke of his burden and the staff of his shoulder, the rod of his oppressor as in the days of Midian.

Absence of the Blessed Sacrament on Good Friday and Easter Eve. 1 Samuel xx. 27, 1 :—Saul said unto Jonathan his son, Wherefore cometh not the Son of Jesse to meat neither yesterday nor to-day?

The same. S. Luke xxiv. 3 :—And they entered in, and found not the Body of the LORD JESUS.

Advent. Exodus iv. 14, 1 :—And also, behold, He cometh forth to meet thee, and when he seeth thee He will be glad in His heart.

Ascension. 2 Chron. i. 13 :—Then Solomon came from His journey to the high place that was at Gibeah to

Jerusalem from before the tabernacle of the congregation and reigned over Israel.

Our Lord's perpetual mediation. Neh. vi. 3 :—And I sent messengers unto them saying, I am doing a great work so that I cannot come down.

Easter-Day. Gen. i. 5, *l* :—And the evening and the morning were the first day.

Christmas. 1 Sam. xx. 6, *m* :—David earnestly asked leave of Me that He might run to Bethlehem, His city.

Easter. 1 Sam. xxv. 29 :—Yet a man is risen to pursue thee, and to seek thy soul, but the soul of my Lord shall be bound in the bundle of life with the LORD thy GOD.

Easter. 1 Sam. xvii. 20 :—And David rose up early in the morning, and left the sheep with a keeper, and took and went as Jesse had commanded Him.

Easter. 1 Sam. xx. 19 :—And when Thou hast stayed three days, then Thou shalt go down quickly, and come to the place where the business was in hand, and remain by the stone Ezel.

Easter. 2 Sam. xxiii. 4 :—And He shall be as the light of the morning, when the sun riseth, even a morning without clouds.

Good Friday. (Jewish ignorance of our LORD). 1 Sam. xvii. 55 :—And when Saul saw David go forth against the Philistine, he said unto Abner, Abner, whose son is this youth? And Abner said, As thy soul liveth, O King, I cannot tell.

Passion Tide. Numbers x. 33 :—And they departed from the Mount of the Lord three days' journey, and the Ark of the Covenant of the LORD went before them in the three days' journey, to find a rest for them.

All Saints. 1 Chron. xii. 33 :—Of Zebulun such as went forth to battle, expert in war, with all instruments of war, fifty thousand which could keep rank; they were not of a double heart.

All Saints. 2 Sam. xxiv. 3 *m* :—Now the LORD thy GOD make the people, how many soever they be are hundredfold.

For one sent on difficult work. Judges xiv. 12 :—And Samson said unto them, I will now put forth a riddle unto you; if ye can certainly declare it me within the seven days of the feast, I will give, &c.

The same. 1 Sam. xiv. 4 :—And between the passages by which Jonathan sought to go over unto the Philistines' garrison, there was a sharp rock on the one side and a sharp rock on the other side.

Crucifixion. Judges ix. 48 :— And Abimelech gat him up to Mount Zalmon, and Abimelech took an axe in his hand, and cut down a bough from the trees and laid it on his shoulder, and said unto the people that were with him, What ye have seen me do, make haste and do as I have done.

Whitsunday. 1 Sam. xxv. 2 :—And there was a man in Maon, and the man was very great, and he had

3000 sheep and 1000 goats, and he was shearing sheep on Carmel.

Beginning of the Passion. 2 Sam. xv. 23 :—And all the country wept with a loud voice, and all the people passed over, the king also himself passed over the brook Kedron, and all the people passed over toward the way of the wilderness.

Spiritual Communion. Num. xviii. 27 :—And this your heave offering shall be reckoned to you as though it were the corn of the threshing-floor and as the fulness of the winepress.

The night of Easter Eve. 1 Sam. xxiv. 4 :—And the men of David said unto him, Behold the day of which the Lord said unto thee, Behold, I will deliver thine enemy into thy hand, that thou mayest do to him that shall seem good unto thee.

Easter Morning. Dan. vi. 19 :—Then the King rose very early in the morning, and went in haste unto the den of lions.

Ascension. 1 Chron. xxix. 22. l :—And they made Solomon, the son of David, King the second time, and anointed him unto the Lord to be the chief governor.

S. John Baptist. Judges vii. 24 :—And Gideon sent messengers throughout all Mount Ephraim, saying, Come down against the Midianites, and take before them the waters unto Bethbara and Jordan.

Easter. 2 Kings xxiii. 22 :—Surely there was not

holden such a passover from the days of the judges that judged Israel, nor in all the days of the Kings of Israel, nor of the Kings of Judah.

Easter. S. John xi. 41, *f*:—Then they took away the stone from the place where the dead was laid.

I have now only to thank those who were kind enough to send me corrections to the list of texts. I could wish that more, who have employed the book, would have done so; for I am perfectly aware that in so great a number of figures many errors must remain still undiscovered.

Sackville College, May 28th, 1866.

This second issue, which its accomplished Editor did not live to complete, is now laid before the public by another hand.

It remains to be said that even the *Promptuarium* of Thomas Hibernicus, rich as it is in mystical interpretations of Holy Scripture, is very far, even in conjunction with S. Antony, from exhausting that mine of devotional thought.

It was my hope to publish, with the co-operation of my dear friend, a much fuller Moral Concordance than the present one, embracing not only the authors there laid under contribution (one of whom it was my chance to bring under his notice), but also texts commented on by those writers, patristic, mediæval, and post-Reformation, who have shown themselves most skilled in the same department. Such are Origen, S. Clement of Alexandria, S. Augustine, Venerable Bede, S. Bernard, Richard of S. Victor, S. Bonaventure, Henry Herph, Denys à Rykol, Matthias Faber, Jeremiah Drexelius, and John Cocceius, not omitting the rich stores in the Illations of the Mozaratic Missal, nor the manuscript sermons left behind by Dr. Neale himself. Such a compilation, bringing the resources of so many devout and original minds to bear on the elucidation of Holy Writ, could hardly have failed to deepen the method of studying the Sacred Books. The fulfilment of the scheme is now distant and doubtful. R. F. L.

Nativity of Our Lady, 1866.

BOOK I.

First Part.

1. *Against sin, absolutely.*
   Job 18. 14 ‖ Prov. 13. 21 *f* | 14. 9 *f* ‖ Is. 52. 2 Ecclus. 21. 2.

2. *Of the weight of sin.*
   Ex. 15. 10 *l* ‖ Ps. 38. 4 ‖ Is. 13. 1 | 58. 6 Jer. 17. 21 ‖ Zech. 5. 7 ‖ S. Matt. 11. 28.

3. *Of the blindness of sin.*
   Ex. 10. 22 ‖ Deut. 16. 19 ‖ Job 5. 14 | 17. 7 21. 17 *f* | 24. 14 | 28. 3 | 36. 32 ‖ Ps. 35. 6 69. 24 *f* | 104. 20 ‖ Is. 5. 30 *l* | 6. 10 | 9. 2 29. 10 | 35. 5 | 42. 19 | 43. 8 | 47. 5 | 50. 3 59. 9 *l* | 60. 2 *f* ‖ Jer. 13. 16 ‖ Lam. 2. 1 | 3. 6, 44 4. 14 *f* ‖ Amos 8. 9 ‖ Zech. 11. 17 *l* ‖ Wis. 5. 6 17 17 *l* ‖ S. John 3. 19 | 9. 39 ‖ Rom. 1. 21 *l* 11. 25 *l* ‖ 1 Cor. 2. 14 ‖ Eph. 4. 17, 18 | 5. 14 ‖ Gal. 3. 1 ‖ 1 S. John 2. 11 ‖ Rev. 3. 17 | 8. 12 *l* | 9. 2 16. 10.

4. *Of the hardness of sin.*
   Ex. 7. 3 ‖ Job 41. 24 ‖ Is. 46. 12 | 48. 4 Jer. 5. 3 *l* 17. 1 | 30. 15 ‖ Ezek. 11. 19 ‖ Acts. 7. 51 ‖ Heb. 3. 8.

5. *Of the chains of sin.*
   Job 18. 8 | 39. 5 ‖ Ps. 2. 3 | 9. 16 *l* | 10. 10 11. 7 | 25. 14 | 57. 7 | 68. 7 *m* | 88. 3 | 116. 14 *l* 124. 6 | 140. 5 | 142 3 *l* ‖ Prov. 5. 22 | 7. 21 29. 5 | Eccles. 7. 26 Is. 5. 18 | 52. 2 | 58. 9 *m* Ezek. 3. 25 ‖ Ecclus. 27. 26, 29 ‖ S. Matt. 21. 2 *l* S. John 11. 44.

6. *Of new devices in sin.*
   Is. 3. 8 Jer. 11. 22 | 21. 12 ‖ Hos. 9. 15.

Second Part.

7. *Of gluttony.*

Gen. 3. 6, 19 | 25. 30 ‖ Ex. 12. 39 | 16. 3
Num. 11. 33 ‖ 1 Sam. 14. 24 ‖ 2 Kings 4. 39
Prov. 23. 1 ‖ Lam. 4. 5 ‖ Hos. 10. 13 ‖ Amos 6. 4
Mic. 6. 14 ‖ Ecclus. 31. 12 ‖ Heb. 13. 9.

8. *Of drunkenness.*

Gen. 9. 21 | 19. 32 ‖ Lev. 10. 9 ‖ 2 Sam. 13. 28
1 Kings 16. 9 | 20. 12, 16 ‖ Eccles. 2. 3 f ‖ Is. 29. 9
Jer. 25. 15 ‖ Dan. 1. 8 | 5. 4 ‖ Hos. 4. 11 ‖ Amos 6. 6
Jud. 12. 20 | 13. 2 ‖ Wis. 2. 6 ‖ Ecclus. 31. 30
1 Tim. 3. 8 ‖ Tit. 1. 7 | 2. 3.

9. *Against gluttony and drunkenness, in common.*

Ex. 32. 6 ‖ Judg. 13. 4 | 16. 25 ‖ Esth. 1. 5, 9
5. 8, 12 | 6. 14 ‖ Prov. 21. 17 | 23. 20 ‖ Is. 22. 13
66. 3 ‖ Jer. 23. 15 ‖ Dan. 5. 1 | 10. 2, 3 | Hos. 4. 18
13. 6 ‖ Ecclus. 18. 30 | 19. 1, 2 | 23. 6 | 29. 21
S. Mark 6. 21 ‖ Rom. 13. 13 ‖ Gal. 5. 21.

10. *Against daintiness in meats.*

Gen. 25. 29 ‖ Num. 11. 4 ‖ 1 Sam. 2. 15
S. Matt. 12. 1 ‖ 1 Tim. 6. 8.

11. *Against those who provoke to excessive eating and drinking.*

Num. 25. 2 ‖ 2 Sam. 13. 27 ‖ Esth. 1. 8 ‖ Ps. 69. 22
Prov. 1. 10 | 23. 7, 29, 30 ‖ Is. 22. 13 | 36. 16
56. 12 ‖ Jer. 35. 5 | 52. 26 —(Jerusalem taken by Nebuzar-adan, the prince of the Cooks.) Amos. 2. 12
Hab. 2. 15 ‖ Wis. 2. 7 ‖ Ecclus. 31. 30 ‖ S. Mark 15. 23
S. Luke 12. 19.

12. *Of temperance, or sobriety.*

Gen. 1. 29 | 2. 17 | 3. 17 ‖ Dan. 1. 16 | 10. 3
Ecclus. 31. 27 | 37. 31 ‖ S. Matt. 5. 6 ‖ Rom. 14. 3 f
1 Tim. 3. 2 | 4. 4 | 5. 23 ‖ 1 S. Pet. 2. 11.

13. *That the flesh must be subdued to the spirit; or of temperance and carnal desires.*

Gen. 21. 8 | 48. 11 ‖ Ex. 26. 1 ‖ Deut. 14. 19 Josh. 15. 18 ‖ Judg. 7. 21 ‖ Cant. 4. 14 *l* ‖ Is. 11. 7 30. 24 ‖ Jer. 31. 4 ‖ Nah. 3. 14 ‖ Ecclus. 18. 30 33. 24 | 39. 26 ‖ S. Mark 1. 6 ‖ S. Luke 15. 8 S. John 19. 39 ‖ Rom. 8. 13 | 12. 1 | 13. 14 1 Cor. 9. 27 ‖ Gal. 5. 24 ‖ 1 S. Pet. 2. 11.

14. *Of fasting.*

Ex. 24. 18 ‖ 1 Kings 19. 8 ‖ Esth. 4. 16 ‖ Is. 58. 3 Joel 2. 12 ‖ Jon. 3. 7 ‖ Tob. 12. 8 ‖ Jud. 8. 6 S. Matt. 6. 17 ‖ 1 Cor. 10. 31.

15. *Against indiscreet fasting.*

Dan. 7. 4 ‖ Ecclus. 31. 28 ‖ 1 Tim. 5. 23.

16. *Of a good feast.*

These seven things are to be observed in eating :—
The fear of God : grace : reading : moderate speed : Few words : glad heart : a part to them that need.

The fear of God—S. Jude 12.
Grace—S. Luke 9. 16 | 22. 19 ‖ 1 Tim. 4. 5.
Reading—S. Matt. 4. 4.
Moderate speed—Eccles. 10. 17 ‖ Acts 2. 15.
Few words—Prov. 23. 2 ‖ Ecclus. 31. 12 ‖ 2 Thess. 3. 12.
Glad heart—Neh. 8. 10 ‖ Esth. 9. 19.
A part to them that need—Ecclus. 35. 10.

17. *Against impurity.*

Gen. 38. 24 ‖ Num. 25. 1 ‖ Deut. 22. 22, 30 ‖ Judg. 19. 24 ‖ 1 Sam. 21. 4 ‖ 2 Sam. 6. 7 ‖ 1 Kings 11. 1 Job 31. 9, 12 | 40. 16 ‖ Prov. 6. 25 | 30. 15 ‖ Jer. 2. 22 ‖ Ezek. 16. 7, 30 ‖ Hos. 4. 18 ‖ Hab. 1. 16 Tob. 4. 12 | 6. 16 ‖ Wis. 2. 9 ‖ Ecclus. 9. 6 | 11. 27 41. 22 | 42. 12 ‖ S. Matt. 5. 28 | 15. 19 ‖ Rom. 1. 29 13. 13 ‖ 1 Cor. 5. 1 | 6. 18 | 7. 2 ‖ Gal. 5. 19 ‖ Eph. 5. 5 Col. 3. 5 ‖ 1 Thess. 4. 3 ‖ Heb. 13. 4 ‖ 2 S. Pet. 2. 12, 13 ‖ Rev. 18. 2 | 22. 15.

(38)

18. *Against covetousness.*

Josh. 7. 21 || 1 Kings 21. 2 || 2 Kings 5. 20
Ecclus. 14. 3 || S. Matt. 27. 5 || Acts 5. 1
1 Tim. 6. 9, 10.

19. *Against the frauds of buyers and sellers.*

Gen. 14. 21 | 37. 28 || Lev. 19. 11 || Deut. 25. 13
Prov. 1. 11 | 20. 10, 14 | 26. 27 || Is. 5. 20 | 24. 2 *m*
Jer. 9. 5 || Hos. 12. 7 || Amos 8. 5 || Nah. 3. 1
Ecclus. 26. 29 | 27. 1 || S. Matt. 8. 20 *f* || Rev. 18. 11
1. 5, 16, 23 *l.*

20. *Against those that keep back the pay of their labourers.*

Lev. 19. 13 || Deut. 24. 15 || Job 31. 16 || Tob. 4. 14
Ecclus. 29. 4 | 34. 20 || S. James 5. 4.

21. *Against theft and thieves.*

Gen. 31. 32 || Ex. 20. 15 | 21. 16 | 22. 4
Lev. 19. 11 || Josh. 7. 1 || Prov. 1. 19 || Is. 1. 23
Hos. 7. 1 || Obad. 5 || Hab. 2. 9 || Tob. 2. 13
Eph. 4. 27.

22. *Against sacrilege.*

Jer. 7. 11 | 12. 10 || Ezek. 44. 7 || Dan. 5. 3
1 Cor. 3. 17.

23. *Against those that keep back tithes.*

Gen. 14. 20 || Ex. 22. 29 | 23. 19 || Num. 31. 28
2 Chron. 31. 5 || Mal. 3. 8, 10 || Tob. 1. 7
S. Matt. 5. 17 || S. Mark 1. 44 || 2 Tim. 2. 6.

24. *Against simony.*

Lev. 10. 1 || Num. 16. 1 || Josh. 7. 24 || Judg. 17. 5
1 Kings 13. 33 | 20. 12 || 2 Kings 5. 26 || 2 Chron. 13. 9
18. 19 || Job 13. 3 | 16. 2 || Prov. 23. 23 | 30. 29
Jer. 20. 2 | 48. 10 || Hab. 2. 12 || 1 Macc. 9. 55
2 Macc. 4. 8 | 11. 3 || S. Matt. 10. 8 | 23. 2
S. John 2. 15 || Acts 8. 18 || Heb. 5. 4.

(39)

25. *Against the four crying sins.*
Oppression—Ex. 22. 27 ‖ Ecclus. 35. 17.
Impurity—Gen. 18. 20 ‖ Joel 3. 3 ‖ S. Jude 7.
Murder—Gen. 4. 10.
Keeping back wages—Job 31. 39 ‖ Ecclus. 34. 21, 22
S. James 5. 4.

26. *That those who have acquired money unjustly, are bound to restore it.*
Ex. 21. 19 | 22. 1, 6 ‖ Lev. 5. 15 | 6. 2 ‖ Num. 5. 6
Prov. 28. 24 ‖ Ecclus. 41. 19 ‖ S. Luke 19. 8.

27. *That riches acquired by theft, fraud, calumny, and falsehood, will not endure; and not only perish themselves, but also destroy their possessor.*
Job 4. 8 | 5. 3 | 8. 22 | 18. 19 | 20. 15 | 21. 17
22. 16 | 24. 18, 24 | 27. 14, 19 ‖ Ps. 109. 11
Eccles. 5. 13 ‖ Is. 5. 8, 24 ‖ Ezek. 15. 7 | 16. 39
21. 31 | 23. 25 | 26. 20 | 33. 25 | 34. 10 ‖ Hos. 2. 9, 12
Amos 3. 11 | 6. 7 ‖ Mic. 1. 15 ‖ Wis. 3. 8 | 4. 3
Ecclus. 23. 25 | 40. 13, 15 | 41. 9.

28. *Against the rich and mighty men of this world.*
Gen. 1. 21 | 9. 2 | 10. 8 | 28. 11 *l* | 40. 14
Job 5. 3 | 15. 21 | 21. 7 | 27. 18 ‖ Ps. 14. 9
Eccles. 6. 2 ‖ Is. 13. 17 | 28. 1 | 40. 4 | 43. 6
Jer. 17. 5 | 48. 1 ‖ Hos. 12. 7 ‖ Joel 1. 5 ‖ Wis. 5. 8
6. 6 *l* ‖ Ecclus. 31. 8 ‖ S. Luke 6. 24 | 8. 14
S. John 14. 30 ‖ S. James 4. 4 | 5. 1.

29. *That it is difficult for a rich man to be saved.*
Ps. 49. 12 ‖ S. Matt. 19. 23 ‖ S. Mark 10. 23
S. Luke 18. 24 ‖ Tim. 6. 9.

30. *That it is lawful to possess riches.*
Gen. 13. 2 | 31. 9 ‖ Job 1. 3 ‖ Prov. 22. 2
1 Tim. 2. 2 | 6. 17.

31. *Against the hope of the wicked.*
   Job 20. 8 | 21. 13, 30 | 24. 20 ‖ Ps. 37. 36 | 40. 5 · Prov. 10. 25 ‖ Eccles. 11. 8 ‖ Is. 28. 15 *l* | 30. 2 33. 1 ‖ Jer. 12. 1 *l* ‖ Wis. 5. 8, 14 ‖ Ecclus. 5. 3.

32. *Against those who put their hope in the help of man.*
   Gen. 26. 2 ‖ Judg. 7. 2 ‖ 1 Sam. 17. 45 2 Chron. 20. 12 | 25. 6, 7 | 32. 7 ‖ Ps. 108. 8 Prov. 25. 19 ‖ Is. 10. 20 | 16. 12 | 30. 1 | 31. 1 36. 6 ‖ Jer. 2. 36 | 17. 5 | 22. 20 | 42. 13 | 48. 13 Lam. 4. 17 ‖ Ezek. 29. 6 ‖ Hos. 5. 13 | 8. 8 Amos. 5. 19 ‖ Judith 9. 7 ‖ 1 Macc. 3. 18 | 9. 7, 17.

33. *That we must not trust in transitory things.*
   2 Chron. 25. 8 ‖ Job 31. 24 ‖ Prov. 11. 28 12. 2 | 28. 26 *f* ‖ Is. 29. 14 ‖ Jer. 9. 4 ‖ Hos. 10. 13. Amos. 6. 1 ‖ Mic. 7. 2, 6 ‖ Ecclus. 14. 18 | 32. 22 1 Cor. 1. 19.

34. *That we must always trust in the* LORD.
   Deut. 33. 29 ‖ 1 Sam. 17. 45 ‖ 2 Chron. 20. 12, 20 Prov. 3. 5 ‖ Is. 40. 31 | 42. 5 | 50. 7 ‖ Jer. 7. 14 17. 7 ‖ Wis. 3. 9 ‖ 2 Cor. 7. 4 ‖ Heb. 4. 16.

35. *Of spiritual riches.*
   Job 22. 23 ‖ Prov. 8. 1 | 10. 4 ‖ Is. 33. 6 Wis. 7. 14 | 8. 5 ‖ Ecclus. 13. 24 | 44. 6 ‖ 1 Tim. 6. 17.

36. *Of the contempt of riches.*
   Tobit 2. 11 ‖ Ecclus. 5. 8 ‖ S. Matt. 10. 23 S. Luke 8. 15 | 9. 25.

37. *Of the commendation of poverty.*
   Is. 48. 10 *f* | 53. 2 | 66. 2 *l* | Eccles. 4. 6 ‖ Job 5. 11 S. Matt. 5. 3 ‖ S. Mark 10. 22 ‖ S. Luke 9. 58.

38. *That the Church increases in spiritual gifts by poverty and adversity.*
   Gen. 41. 52 ‖ Ps. 87. 1 ‖ Is. 14. 30, 32 *l* | 30. 20 Ecclus. 10. 10, 30 | 11. 12 ‖ Acts 4. 32 ‖ 2 Cor. 8. 9 Eph. 2. 20 ‖ 1 S. Pet. 2. 4 ‖ Rev. 2. 9.

39. *Of those who trample upon the world.*
    Josh. 1. 3. | 10. 24. || Judg. 5. 21
    Ecclus. 24. 6

40. *Of the misery and labour of human life.*
    Gen. 3. 16 | 8. 21 *l* || Job. 13. 25 | 14. 1
    Eccles 2. 11, 16, 23 | 3. 10 | 6. 7 || Ecclus. 40. 1
    Eph. 5. 15.

41. *Against avarice and covetousness, and its effects:—*
    It brings anxiety—Eccles. 2. 11, 18 | S. Luke 12. 17.
    It causes disturbance—Prov. 11. 29. || Eccles. 2, 22
      Hab. 2. 9, 10.
    It pollutes—Lam. 4. 8 || Hos. 9. 9 || Hab. 2. 6
      Ecclus. 13. 1.
    It condemns—Prov. 1. 32 | 21. 7 || S. Luke 16. 22
      S. James 5. 1.
    It weighs down—Zech. 5. 7 || Wis. 5. 7.
    It puffs up—Job. 24. 24.
    It casts down—Ps. 73. 17 || Prov. 11. 28.
    It blinds—Gen. 20. 16 | Ecclus. 20. 29.
    It spoils—Rev. 3. 17.
    It empties—Is. 29. 8 || S. Luke 1. 53.
    It binds—Job 18. 8 | 1 Tim. 6. 9.
    It afflicts—Ecclus. 4. 8 | 5. 13 | 10. 15.
    It closes paradise—S. Mark 10. 24 || S. Luke 18. 24.
    It is the mother of all crimes—Ecclus. 10. 9 | 27. 1
      1 Tim. 6. 10.
    It makes God our enemy—S. James 4. 4.
    It breaks down the defences of the mind || Hab. 1. 10.
    It seduces with the appearance of kindness—S.
      Matt. 26. 48 || 1 Thess. 5. 5.
    It chokes the words of Salvation—S. Matt. 13. 22
      S. Luke 8. 7.
    It deceives—Job 27. 19 || Ps. 76. 5 | S. Matt. 13. 22
      S. Mark 4. 19.
    It torments—Gen. 31. 40 || Eccles. 2. 23.
    It conquers—Eccles. 6. 10 | 10. 19.

It causes men to backslide—Hos. 9. 3. | 12. 1.
It causes the Holy Ghost to withdraw Himself—Hos. 5. 6 || S. Matt. 6. 24.
It speedily passes away—Ecclus. 40. 13.
It destroys love—1 S. John 2. 15.
It profits not in the hour of death—Prov. 6. 35 10. 2 | 11. 4 || Ezek. 7. 19.
It separates from Christ—Jer. 7. 24 || Ezek. 7. 25 Zeph. 1. 18.
It brings into danger—Prov. 21. 6 | 28. 20 || Is. 59. 5. Hos. 8. 6 || Hab. 2. 9.
It does not increase good works—S. Mark 12. 42 S. Luke 21. 2.
It is the parent of folly—Eccles. 10. 15. || S. Luke 12. 20.
Of lies—Hos. 7. 1 || Ecclus. 25. 2.
Of fear—Gen. 4. 15 || Job 15. 21 || Ps. 89. 41 Is. 24. 17.
Of rapacity—1 Kings 21. 15 || Prov. 1. 19 || Wis. 15. 12.
It mocks at the righteous—Job 12. 4 || Ecclus. 27. 1.
Its prayers are not heard—Job 27. 9.
It heaps up the anger of God—Job 12. 6 || Is. 57. 17 Hos. 12. 14 || Zech. 1. 15 || S. James 5. 3.
It chooses the bitter instead of the sweet—Job 30. 7 Prov. 23. 35 | 27. 6.
It is not sensible of wounds—Job 33. 20 || Prov. 23. 35 || Is. 42. 25 || Jer. 5. 3.
It despises wholesome doctrine—Job 33. 20 || Prov. 27. 7 || Jer. 22. 21.
It despises the poor—Amos 6. 6 || Ecclus. 13. 24 S. Luke 16. 24.
It is terrified at death—Ecclus. 41. 1.
It can scarcely be amended—Jer. 8. 6 | 48. 11 Hos. 7. 8 | 13. 12 || Ecclus. 31. 5.
It heaps up wealth for others—Job 1. 21 | 5. 5 20. 15 | 27. 16, 17 || Ps. 49. 11, 18 || Prov. 13 22 *l* 22. 16 || Eccles. 2. 18, 26 *m* || Jer. 17. 11.
It causes sloth—Jer. 48. 11.

Rebellion—Deut. 32. 15 ‖ Jer. 5. 27 ‖ Hos. 7. 15.
Weakness—Jer. 46. 5.
Hatred—Prov. 11. 26 ‖ S. James 4. 4.
Idolatry—Hos. 8. 4 | 10. 1 ‖ Col. 3. 5.
Hardness of heart—Job 41. 24 ‖ Is. 48. 4 ‖ Zech. 7. 12.
Oblivion—Prov. 10. 7.

42. *Against hardness of heart.*
Deut. 15. 7 ‖ Job 23. 16 | 30. 25 ‖ Prov. 28. 14 *l*
Jer. 5. 3 ‖ Amos 6. 6 ‖ Zech. 7. 12 ‖ Ecclus. 43. 20
1 Cor. 12. 26. ‖ Gal. 6. 2 ‖ 1 Tim. 5. 8 ‖ 1 S. John 3. 14.

43. *Against those that are unwilling to lend.*
Ex. 22. 25 ‖ Lev. 25. 25 ‖ Deut. 15. 9 | 23. 20
Ps. 37. 21 ‖ S. Matt. 5. 42.

44. *Of the mercy of the* LORD ; *or of the sweetness of* GOD'S *loving kindness towards the Poor.*
Gen. 6. 3 | 18. 7, 32 | 19. 12, 22, 26 | 21. 17
26. 2. 3 | 28. 12 | 31. 24 | 32. 26 ‖ Ex. 3. 7
6. 6 | 9. 26 | 10. 23 | 11. 7 | 14. 30 | 23. 22
34. 6 ‖ Num. 20. 8 ‖ Deut. 10. 18 | 28. 5 | 32. 6, 10
33. 3 *f* ‖ Josh. 6. 20 ‖ Judg. 4. 3 | 10. 16 *l*
2 Sam. 24. 14 ‖ Ps. 7. 12 | 9. 10, 13 | 11. 5 | 12. 6
17. 7 | 18. 6, 16, 27 | 31. 21 | 32. 6 | 33. 17
34. 6, 18 | 36. 7 *f* | 37. 5, 23, 24, 40 | 41. 2 | 44. 8
48. 8 | 49. 15 | 51. 1 | 54. 7 | 57. 1 | 58. 10 *f*
63. 4 | 66. 14 | 69. 14 | 72. 12 | 73. 22
86. 5, 13, 15 | 89. 1, 48 | 91. 4, 11 | 94. 18, 19
100. 4 | 103. 3, 8 | 105. 12, 38 | 106. 1, 4
107. 1, 8, 43 | 109. 20 | 111. 4 | 113. 5 | 116. 5
118. 1 | 130. 8 | 140. 7 | 143. 10 | 144. 2 | 145. 7
147. 3 ‖ Is. 30. 19 *m* | 40. 11 | 49. 15 | 57. 18
61. 1 | 63. 7 | 64. 5 ‖ Jer. 3. 12 *l* | 15. 19 | 29. 13
31. 18 *l* ‖ Ezek. 18. 23 ‖ Dan. 9. 18 ‖ Hos. 6. 4
14. 5 ‖ Joel 2. 12 ‖ Jon. 4. 2 *l* ‖ Zech. 1. 3, 16
Mal. 3. 7 ‖ Ecclus. 2. 11 | 5. 4 *l* | 18. 5 | 24. 20
35. 20 ‖ S. Matt. 5. 44 | 8. 7 | 9. 2, 36 | 11. 28, 29
14. 27 | 15. 28 | 18. 21, 22, 27 | 20. 34 | 23. 37
S. Luke 15. 4, 22 ‖ Rom. 2. 4.

45. *Of the grace of* God.

Prov. 12. 2 ‖ Ecclus. 40. 17 ‖ S. Matt. 10. 8 S. John 1. 17 | 15. 5 | Rom. 6. 15, 23 | 12. 6 1 Cor. 12. 4 | 15. 10 ‖ 2 Cor. 9. 8 | 11. 7 ‖ Gal. 2. 21 Eph. 2. 7, 8 ‖ 1 Tim. 4. 4, 14 ‖ Heb. 4. 16.

46. *Of the union of mercy and justice.*

Gen. 24. 49 ‖ Ps. 7. 12 | 25. 7, 9 | 26. 3 | 36. 5 57. 4, 11 | 61. 7 | 84. 12 | 89. 25, 33 | 92. 2 101. 1 | 108. 4 | 117. 2 | 138. 2 *m* ‖ Prov. 3. 3 14. 22 | 16. 6 | 19. 12 | 20. 28 ‖ Nah. 1. 3 Mal. 1. 6.

47. *Of the commendation of mercy.*

Ex. 25. 17 ‖ Job 29. 6 ‖ Ps. 84. 12 | 42. 8 Cant. 1. 3 ‖ Hos. 6. 6 | Zech. 1. 16 *f*.

48. *Of the mercy of man.*

Ex. 25. 2 ‖ Job 6. 14 ‖ Prov. 14. 21 | 22. 9 Eccles. 11. 4 ‖ Is. 58. 7 ‖ Hos. 6. 6 | 10. 12 Ecclus. 14. 13 | 18. 16 | 28. 2 | 29. 1 | 30. 24 S. Luke 6. 30 | 9. 60 ‖ 2 Cor. 9. 7 ‖ 1 Tim. 4. 7.

49. *Of compassion.*

2 Sam. 1. 17 | 3. 31 ‖ Job 5. 18 | 30. 25 Eccles. 7. 3 ‖ Is. 22. 4 | 24. 16 *m* ‖ Jer. 9. 1 | 13. 17 Amos. 6. 6 ‖ S. Matt. 15. 32 ‖ S. Luke 19. 41 S. John 11. 33 ‖ Rom. 12. 15 ‖ 1 Cor. 12. 26 2 Cor. 7. 3 | 11. 29 ‖ Gal. 6. 3.

50. *Of a good will in almsgiving; or, that* God *considers not how much, but from how much.*

Gen. 4. 5 | 43. 11 ‖ Prov. 11. 20 ‖ Is. 1. 15 Hos. 5. 6 ‖ Ecclus. 34. 20 | 35. 6 ‖ S. Matt. 10. 42 S. Mark 12. 43 ‖ S. John 9. 41 ‖ 2 Cor. 8. 10 9. 2, 7 *l*.

51. *Of liberality.*

 Esth. 2. 18 || Job 31. 17 || Ecclus. 4. 31 || S. Matt. 12. 13 || S. Luke 6. 30, 38 *f.*

52. *Of almsgiving.*

 Pure, frequent, hearty, moderate and free;
 To whom, how much, what, how, when, why from thee.

Pure—Ex. 27. 20 || Lev. 24. 2 || Acts 10. 2.
Frequent—Eccles. 11. 6.
Hearty—Ps. 112 2 || Rev. 2. 19.
Moderate—2 Cor. 8. 13, 14.
And free—2 Cor. 6. 12.
To whom—Prov. 13. 8.
How much—S. Luke 11. 41 || 1 Tim. 6. 8.
What—Tob. 4. 7.
How—Ecclus. 18. 15.
When—Prov. 3. 28 || Ecclus. 4. 1.
Why from thee—S. Matt. 6. 2.

53. *Of almsgiving in general.*

 Deut. 15. 7, 11 || Job 31. 16 || Prov. 3. 9 | 11. 24. 17. 1 | 19. 17 | 28. 27 | 31. 20 || Is. 55. 10 | 58. 10. Jer. 2. 21 || Ecclus. 3. 14 | 4. 1 | 14. 13 | 20.12 | 29. 12 S. Matt. 25. 34 || S. Mark 4. 26 | 12. 42 || S. Luke 3. 11 6. 30, 38 | 12. 33 | 16. 9 | 19. 8 || 1 Cor. 9. 11 15. 42 *l* | 16. 1 || 2 Cor. 8. 2, 12 | 9. 6 || Gal. 6. 8 Eph. 4. 28 || Heb. 13. 1, 16.

54. *Of the effects of almsgiving.*

It turns away the wrath of God—Prov. 21. 14 Ecclus. 3. 30.
It sets free—Tob. 4. 10.
It cleanses—S. Luke 11. 41.
It redeems—Dan. 4. 27.
It brings a blessing—Acts 10. 4.
It makes perfect—S. Matt. 19. 21.
It blesses—Deut. 24. 19.

It heals—Prov. 13. 8 | 16. 6.
It raises—Acts 9. 40.
It arms—Ecclus. 29. 13.
It increases—S. Luke 18. 29, 30.
It strengthens—Tob. 4. 11.
It enlightens—Ecclus—7. 20 ‖ Acts 10. 3.
It enlarges—Prov. 3. 9, 10 | 11. 24, 25 | 18. 16
   28. 27 ‖ 2 Cor. 9. 6, 10.
It anoints—S. Luke 7. 46.

55. *That alms are to be given with cheerfulness.*
Ecclus. 18. 15 | 35. 10 *l* ‖ 2 Cor. 9. 7 *l*.

56. *To whom alms are to be given; and that they are not to be given to those who need them not.*
Ps. 112. 9 ‖ Is. 58. 7 ‖ Jer. 4. 3 ‖ Ecclus. 12. 1, 2, 4 S. Luke 14. 12.

57. *Against those who offer to* God *the worst of that which they have.*
Gen. 43. 11 ‖ Mal. 1. 8, 14.

58. *That alms are to be given in our life-time.*
Ps. 95. 2 ‖ Is. 58. 7 ‖ Ezek. 1. 12. ‖ S. Matt. 19. 21 Philip. 3. 13.

59. *That alms, given from robbery, are not acceptable to* God.
1 Chron. 21. 24. ‖ 2 Chron. 31. 3 ‖ Prov. 3. 9 15. 8 | 21. 27 ‖ Ecclus. 34. 18 | 35. 12 ‖ 1 Tim. 6. 5 *l*.

60. *That the offerings of the wicked will not be accepted.*
Deut. 23. 18 ‖ Is. 1. 13 ‖ Jer. 6. 20 | 14. 12 *f* Amos 5. 22 ‖ S. Matt. 5. 23.

61. *That the oblation of a righteous man is acceptable to* God.
Gen. 4. 4 ‖ Ps. 51. 17 ‖ Ecclus. 35. 6, 7.

62. *Of visiting the poor, and of hospitality.*

    Gen. 18. 3 | 19. 1 | 23. 9 | 29. 13 || Deut. 10. 19
Josh. 2. 1 || Job. 5. 24 || S. Luke 1. 39 || Heb. 13. 2
S. James 1. 27 || 1 S. Pet. 4. 9.

63. *Of visiting the sick.*

    Job 29. 25 || Is. 38. 1 | 61. 1 || Ecclus. 7. 34
38. 9 || S. Matt. 25. 43 || 2 Cor. 1. 7 || S. James 1. 27.

64. *Of the works of mercy.*

Visit : give meat : give drink : redeem the slave :
Clothe : house the stranger : lay the dead in grave.

  Visit—Ecclus. 38. 9 || S. Matt. 25. 36.
  Give meat—Prov. 25. 21 || Rom. 12. 20.
  Give drink—S. Matt. 10. 42.
  Redeem the slave—Jer. 38. 10 || S. Matt. 25. 36
    2 Tim. 1. 16.
  Clothe—Is. 58. 7 *l*.
  House the stranger—Gen. 19. 2 || Job 31. 32
    Is. 58. 7 *m*.
  Lay the dead in grave—Tob. 1. 17.

Counsel : rebuke : instruct in wisdom's way :
Console : forgive : endure unmoved : and pray.

  Counsel—Ex. 18. 14 || Rev. 3. 18.
  Rebuke—S. James 5. 20.
  Instruct in wisdom's way—Deut. 4. 10 || 1 Sam. 12. 23.
  Console—Job 30. 25 || 2 Cor. 11. 29.
  Forgive—Ecclus. 28. 2.
  Endure unmoved—Acts 20. 24 || 1 Cor. 13. 7 *f*.
  And pray—Num. 12. 13 || Job 42. 8 *m* || S. James
    5. 16.

65. *Against pride and its effects.*

    It casts down—Job 30. 22, 23 || Ps. 83. 13
Prov. 29. 23 || Eccles. 10. 7 || Is. 15. 12
S. Luke 1. 52 | 6. 37.

It infatuates—Prov. 21. 24 ‖ Jer. 49. 16 ‖ Hab. 2. 5.
It condemns—Is. 2. 12 ‖ Jer. 50. 31.
It depresses—Is. 28. 3 ‖ Mic. 1. 3 ‖ Ecclus. 11. 6.
It is the mother of all crimes—Ecclus. 10. 13 *f.*
It destroys virtue—Is. 28. 4 ‖ Ecclus. 6. 22.
It pollutes all good—1 Cor. 5. 6.
It stirs up quarrels—Prov. 13. 10 ‖ 28. 25 ‖ Ecclus. 27. 15.
It closes paradise—Ps. 101. 7 ‖ Tob. 4. 13 *m.*
It causes scandals—Prov. 22. 5 ‖ Ecclus. 27. 28.
Idolatry—S. John 5. 44.
Hatred—Ps. 74. 24.
It spoils wealth—Ecclus. 21. 4 *l.*
It is rarely cured—Prov. 26. 12 ‖ Ecclus. 3. 28.
It hinders from beholding CHRIST—S. John 5. 44.
It quickly passes—Job 15. 20 | 24. 24, 1 Macc. 2. 63.
It subdues the heart to Satan—Job 41. 34.
It takes the cloak of virtue—Is. 47. 10 ‖ Ezek. 22. 5.
It causes hypocrisy—S. Matt. 23. 12, 13 ‖ S. Luke 20. 47.
It oppresses the innocent—Ps. 119. 78.
It despises the poor—S. James 2. 3.
Superiors.—Gen. 16. 5   1 Sam. 1. 6.
Inferiors—S. Luke 18. 11.
It seeks the first place—S. Matt. 23. 6   " S. Luke 20. 46 | 22. 24.
It cannot serve—Job 21. 15   Isaiah 14. 13.
It is Satan's offspring—S. John 8. 44.
——————— host—Job 40. 21.
——————— food—Job 40. 15 *f*   S. James 1. 10.
It is impatient—Prov. 6. 16, 17.
Hateful—Ecclus. 10. 7 | 25. 2.
Accursed—Is. 21. 1   Amos 6. 8   Ecclus. 10. 13.

66. *Causes of pride.*

Beauty—Ezek. 28. 2.
Strength—Ecclus. 40. 26.
Power—S. Luke 1. 52.

Riches—Deut. 8. 12.
Dignity—Deut. 17. 20.
Outward ornament—Ecclus. 11. 4.

67. *Of pride in common.*
Gen. 11. 2, 7 ‖ Lev. 1. 16 ‖ Deut. 1. 43 | 17. 12
1 Sam. 2. 3 ‖ 2 Kings 18. 4 ƒ | Job 11. 12 | 15. 13
20. 6, 7 | 35. 12 | 36. 19 | 38. 15 | 39. 18 | 41. 25
Ps. 129. 4 | 131. 1 ‖ Prov. 8. 13 | 11. 2 | 16. 18
18. 12 | 20. 23 | 21. 24 | 25. 6 | 29. 23 | Is. 2. 10
5. 14 | 10. 12 *l*, 33 | 13. 19 | 14. 12, 15 | 16. 6
22. 16 | 23. 7 | 24. 21 | 30. 31 | 34 5. | 37. 23, 29
40. 4ƒ | 47. 8 ‖ Jer. 48. 29 | 50. 31 | 51. 13 ‖ Ezek. 6. 3
7. 10 | 16. 49 | 28. 2 ‖ Dan. 4. 30 | 5 20 ‖ Obad. 3, 4
Hab. 2. 5 | Mal. 4. 1 ‖ Ecclus. 10. 7, 9, 14 | 16. 8
32. 18 *m* ‖ 2 Macc. 9 4 *l*, 7 | 15. 6 ‖ S. Luke 1. 52
10. 18 | 14. 11 ‖ 2 Thess. 2. 4 ‖ S. James 4. 6
2 S. Pet. 2. 4, 18 ‖ Rev. 14. 8 | 18. 7.

68. *Against those that boast themselves of their beauty.*
2 Sam. 14. 25 ‖ Prov. 11. 22 | 31. 30 ‖ Ezek. 28. 17
S. John 6. 63.

69. *Against those that boast themselves of their knowledge.*
Prov. 21. 30 ‖ Ecclus. 41. 15, 20.

70. *Against those that boast themselves of their strength.*
Is. 10. 13 ‖ Jer. 9. 23 *m* ‖ Wis. 6. 8.

71. *Against those that boast themselves of their rank.*
Job. 17. 14 ‖ Ezek. 25. 13 ‖ Mal. 2. 10.

72. *Against those that boast themselves in their riches.*
Job 21. 7 ‖ Ps. 37. 7, 36 | 49. 6, 17 ‖ Jer. 9. 23
Zech. 11. 5 ‖ S. Luke 12. 18.

73. *Of humility and its effects.*
It instructs—Prov. 11. 2 *l*.
It enriches—Prov. 31. 29.

It gives wisdom—Ps. 119. 136 ‖ S. Matt. 11. 25.
It opens the gate of paradise—Rev. 3. 8.
It clothes the naked—Ps. 45. 10.

74. *Of humility in general.*

Gen. 5. 30 | 18. 27 | 46. 32 ‖ Ex. 3. 11 | 4. 10
Judg. 6. 15 ‖ 1 Sam. 9. 21 | 15. 17 | 17. 32 | 18. 23
24. 14 ‖ 2 Sam. 6. 22. ‖ 1 Kings 3. 7 | 21. 29
2 Chron. 12. 7 ‖ Job 22. 29 | 42. 5 ‖ Ps. 10. 13
34. 18 | 51. 17 | 65. 14 | 78. 70 | 84. 11 | 102. 17
113. 5 | 131. 1 | 138. 6 ‖ Prov. 25. 6 | 30. 28
Cant. 2. 1 ‖ Is. 8. 6 | 40. 4 | 66. 2 *l* | Jer. 1. 6
Ezek. 1. 25 ‖ Amos 7. 14 ‖ Zech. 9. 9 *l* ‖ Wis. 6. 7 *l*
Ecclus. 3. 20 | 11. 1, 12 *l* | 13. 1 | 20. 11 | 35. 17 *f*
Bar. 2. 18 ‖ 1 Macc. 9. 73 ‖ S. Matt. 3. 11, 15
4. 19 | 5. 3 | 11. 29 | 18. 3 | 19. 14 | 21. 5 | 23. 11
S. Luke 1. 38, 48 | 2. 51 | 7. 38 | 14. 8 | 18. 13
22. 27 ‖ S. John 5. 9 | 13. 5 | 20. 17 ‖ Acts 9. 5
10. 26 ‖ Rom. 12. 16 ‖ 1 Cor. 1. 27 | 15. 9
Philip. 2. 3. 8 ‖ Col. 3. 12 ‖ Heb. 11. 23 ‖ S. James 1, 21
4. 6 *l* ‖ Rev. 19. 10.

75. *That he who would ascend to virtues, must first descend by humility.*

1 Sam. 2. 8 ‖ Job. 22. 29 ‖ Prov. 15. 33 | 29. 23 *l*
Ecclus. 10. 14 | 11. 1 ‖ S. Matt. 18. 4 ‖ S. Luke 1. 48, 52
14. 8 | 17. 14 | 1 S. Pet. 5. 6.

76. *That the* LORD *hath chosen the weak things of the world.*

1 Sam. 15. 17 ‖ 2 Sam. 7. 8 ‖ Ps. 78. 71 ‖ Amos. 7. 15
S. Matt. 4. 18 ‖ 1 Cor. 1. 27.

77. *That he who is perfect ought to consider himself imperfect.*

Ex. 39. 25 ‖ Job 31. 24 ‖ Ps. 26. 11 | 70. 5
Prov. 8. 34 ‖ Cant. 3. 6 ‖ Joel 1. 1 ‖ Ecclus. 18. 7
S. Luke 17. 10 ‖ S. John 19. 39 ‖ Philip. 3. 13.

78. *He that compares himself to his superiors is humbled.*
   1 Sam. 21. 17 ‖ S. Luke 1. 43 | 3. 16 ‖ Acts 10. 25
   1 Cor. 15. 9.

79. *He that compares himself to his inferiors is made proud.*
   S. Luke 18. 11 ‖ Acts 11. 2.

80. *That our righteousness, compared with the righteousness of* God, *is nothing.*
   Gen. 18. 27 | 19. 23 ‖ Ex. 3. 6 | 4. 10, Job 9. 2, 20
   22. 2 | 25. 4 | 42. 5 ‖ Prov. 20. 9 ‖ Cant. 4. 11
   Is. 6. 5 | 38. 14 | 43. 26 | 64. 6 ‖ Jer. 2. 22 | 7. 4
   Lam. 4. 20 ‖ Rom. 7. 18 ‖ Heb. 12. 3 ‖ 1 S. John 1. 10.

81. *Of the false humility of the proud.*
   Ex. 9. 27 | 10. 16 ‖ Josh. 7. 20 ‖ Judg. 1. 7
   1 Sam. 15. 24, 30 ‖ Esth. 7. 7 ‖ Prov. 26. 25
   Is. 29. 4 ‖ Ecclus. 12. 11 | 19. 26 | 29. 5 2 Macc. 9.
   11, 17, 26 ‖ S. Matt. 27. 4 ‖ Acts 8. 24 ‖ Rev. 3. 15.

82. *Of obedience and its commendation.*
   Gen. 12. 4 | 17. 23 | 21. 14 | 22. 3. 16 | 24. 45
   28. 6 ‖ Num. 32. 25 ‖ Deut. 28. 1 | 29. 9 | 30. 2
   Josh. 10. 12, 13 | 11. 15 ‖ Judg. 8. 24, 25
   1 Sam. 3. 5, 16 | 15. 22 *l* ‖ 1 Kings 19. 19
   Esth. 2. 20 ‖ Ps. 119. 4 ‖ Prov. 13. 13 | 19. 16
   Eccles. 8. 5 *f* ‖ · Is. 11. 14 *l* | 20. 2 | 58. 13
   Ecclus. 3. 1 ‖ 1 Macc. 2. 65 | 8. 16 ‖ S. Matt. 21. 31
   23. 3 ‖ S. Luke 2. 51 ‖ Acts 5. 29 | 9. 6 ‖ Rom. 5. 19
   13. 1 ‖ 1 Cor. 11. 2 ‖ Eph. 6. 1 ‖ Col. 3. 20
   2 Thess. 3. 4, 14 ‖ 1 Tim. 3. 4 ‖ Tit. 3. 1 ‖ Philem 21.
   Heb. 11. 8 | 13. 17 ‖ 1 S. Pet. 1. 14, 22 | 2. 13
   3. 6 | 5. 5.

83. *Against those that are disobedient.*
   Gen. 3. 17 ‖ Num. 16. 12 ‖ Deut. 17. 12 | 21. 18
   1 Sam. 15. 23 ‖ 1 Kings 13. 21 | 20. 36 ‖ Job 36. 12
   Jer. 6. 19 ‖ Hos. 10. 3 ‖ 2 Thess. 1. 8 ‖ Tit. 1. 10
   2 S. Pet. 2. 10.

84. *That we are to obey wicked superiors in that which they command, if it be consistent with* GOD's *Will.*
S. Matt. 23. 3 ‖ 1 S. Pet. 2. 18.

85. *That we are not to obey good superiors when they command that which is contrary to* GOD's *Law.*
2 Macc. 7. 30 ‖ Acts 5. 29.

86. *Against vain glory.*
Lev. 3. 17 ‖ 1 Sam. 13. 3 ‖ Job 15. 2 ‖ Ps. 52. 1
74. 5 | 97. 7 | 131. 1 ‖ Prov. 27. 1 ‖ Jer. 9. 23
Ezek. 7. 10 | 16. 49 ‖ Dan. 4. 30 | 5. 20 ‖ Obad. 4
Zeph. 1. 7 ‖ Ecclus. 6. 2 | 7. 4 ‖ S. Matt. 6. 1
23. 13 ‖ S. Luke 1. 29 | 10. 20 ‖ S. John 8. 50
12. 43 ‖ Rom. 3. 27 ‖ 1 Cor. 1. 27 ‖ 2 Cor. 10. 18
11. 18 | 12. 1, 5 ‖ Gal. 5. 26 | 6. 13 ‖ Philip. 2. 3.

87. *Against foolish mirth.*
Judges 16. 25 *l* | 1 Sam. 30. 16 ‖ 1 Kings 1. 49
Job 20. 5 ‖ Eccles. 1. 2 | 2. 2 | 7. 3 | 11. 9
Jer. 9. 1, 18 | 52. 4 ‖ Lam. 4. 21. ‖ Dan. 5. 5
Joel 1. 8, 13 | 2. 12 ‖ Wis. 5. 8 ‖ Ecclus. 5. 4 | 7. 36
16. 1 | 21. 20 | 22. 6 | 23. 2 ‖ Bar. 4. 26 ‖ 1 Macc. 6. 11
9. 41 ‖ 2 Macc. 9. 8 ‖ S. Matt. 5. 5 | 24. 38
S. James 4. 9 | 5. 1 ‖ Rev. 18. 7.

88. *Of the shortness of the present life, and the vanity of man; or, against those that presume on a long life.*
Gen. 3. 19 | 6. 3 | 19. 27 | 47. 9 ‖ 2 Sam. 14. 14
1 Chron. 19. 15 ‖ Job 4. 18 | 7. 1, 7 | 9. 25 | 10. 20
13. 25 | 14. 1, 10, 20 | 15. 33 | 17. 1 | 18. 5 | 20. 4
21. 13, 18 | 24. 24 | 25. 6 | 27. 19 | 30. 19 *l*
Ps. 37. 2. 37 | 58. 8 | 76. 5 | 90. 6 | 102. 3
103. 14, 15 ‖ Eccles. 2. 11, 23 | 5. 15 | 11. 8 | 12. 7
Is. 16. 9 | 24. 7 | 28. 1 | 29. 5 | 40. 6 | 41. 29
47. 7 | 51. 6 ‖ Jer. 16. 9 | 25. 10 ‖ Dan. 4. 26
5. 30 ‖ Hos. 2. 11 | 10. 7 | 13. 3 ‖ Jon. 4. 7
Zech. 4. 10 ‖ Wis. 2. 1. 5 | 5. 9, 14 ‖ Ecclus. 11. 19
14. 12, 18 | 17. 31 | 18. 9 | 21. 9 | 28. 7 | 38. 22
40. 1, 11 ‖ S. Matt. 6. 30 ‖ Acts 12. 21 ‖ 1 Cor. 7. 31
S. James 4. 14 ‖ Rev. 18. 17.

(53)

89. *Against hypocrites and by what signs they are known.*
2. Sam. 15. 2 ‖ Job 20. 5 | 36. 13 | 39. 13 Ps. 49. 13 ‖ Prov. 9. 17 | 11. 9 | 26. 24 ‖ Is. 3. 3, 14 58. 4 ‖ Jer. 2. 33 | Zech. 13. 4 | Ecclus. 1. 29 12. 11 | 19. 26 2 Macc. 13. 3 ‖ S. Matt. 6. 2, 5 7. 5, 15 | 12. 32 | 23. 13 ‖ S. Mark 12. 38 S. Luke 11. 43 | 12. 1 | 20. 46 Acts 23. 3 | 24. 26 2 Cor. 11. 13 ‖ 1 Tim. 4. 1.

90. *Against those that observe the lesser commandments and neglect the greater.*
Gen. 27. 22 ‖ Mal. 1. 14 S. Matt. 23. 23 S. Luke 11. 42.

91. *That they who have secretly committed some great sin, cannot long escape detection, through the just judgment of* God.
Josh. 7. 18 ‖ 2 Sam. 12. 12 ‖ 2 Kings 5. 25 S. Matt. 10. 26 ‖ S. Luke 8. 17 | 12. 2 ‖ Acts 5. 1 1 Tim. 5. 25.

92. *Of a good or evil intention.*
Eccles. 2. 14 ‖ S. Matt. 6. 23 S. Luke 11. 34 1 Cor. 10. 31 ‖ Col. 3. 17.

93. *That all good works are to be done for the sake of* God, *and not for the sake of temporal benefits.*
Ex. 12. 8 ‖ Lev. 2. 11 Ps. 49. 18 ‖ S. Matt. 6. 6, 33 ‖ S. Luke 22. 19 *l* ‖ S. John 4. 24 ‖ Col. 3. 2.

94. *That all good gifts are to be attributed to* God; *and that He is to be praised for them.*
Job 31. 25 ‖ Eccles. 1. 7 *l* ‖ Is. 26. 12 *l* ‖ Zech. 6. 11 ‖ 1 Cor. 3. 6 | 15. 10 ‖ Philip. 2. 13 ‖ Rev. 4. 5.

95. *That we are not to seek the favour of man in our works.*
Gen. 31. 20 | 1 Sam. 14. 1 Is. 39. 4 *l* Jer. 48. 10 | S. Matt. 6. 1 | 8. 4 *f* | 17. 9 ‖ S. Mark 9. 9 S. John 8. 50.

96. *Against those who ascribe their works to their own strength.*
  Is. 10. 13,15 ‖ Dan. 4. 30 ‖ 1 Cor. 4. 7.

97. *That we ought to hide our good works.*
  Gen. 31. 20 ‖ Ex. 2. 2 ‖ Deut. 15. 19 ‖ Is. 39. 2 ‖ Jer. 20. 15 ‖ S. Matt. 5. 3.

98. *Against anger and its effects.*
  It expels the gifts of GOD—Heb. 12. 15.
  It murders—Job 5. 2 | 18. 4 ‖ S. Matt. 5. 22 ‖ Gal. 5. 20.
  It grieves the HOLY GHOST—Eph. 4. 30.
  It causes strife—Prov. 15. 18 | 26. 21 | 30. 33 ‖ Ecclus. 28. 11.
  It is hateful—Prov. 27. 3 ‖ Ecclus. 27. 30.
  It blinds—Job 17. 7.
  It opens a door to the devil—Eph. 4. 26.
  It can look for no mercy—Prov. 27. 4 ‖ S. Matt. 5. 7.

99. *Against anger in general.*
  Gen. 4. 5 | 13. 7, 8 | 26. 20 | 31. 29 | 34. 7, 25 | 40. 1 | 44. 18 ‖ Ex. 2. 13 | 21. 18 ‖ Lev. 3. 3 ‖ Num. 22. 27 | 24. 10 ‖ 1 Sam. 18. 8 ‖ 2 Sam. 19. 42 ‖ Esth. 3. 5 ‖ Job 36. 18 ‖ Ps. 37. 8 ‖ Prov. 15. 18 | 17. 1 | 18. 14 | 19. 12 | 20. 3 | 21. 9, 19 | 22. 8, 24 | 27. 3 ‖ Eccles. 11. 10 ‖ Dan. 3. 19 ‖ Wis. 10. 3 ‖ Ecclus. 1. 22 | 8. 11 | 22. 14 | 28. 3 | 40. 5 ‖ S. Matt. 5. 5 ‖ Rom. 12. 19 | 1 Cor. 13. 4 ‖ Eph. 6. 4 ‖ Col. 3. 8 ‖ S. James 1. 20.

100. *That anger must not gain dominion over the mind.*
  Job 36. 18 ‖ Ecclus 40. 4 ‖ Eph. 4. 26.

101. *Against impatience.*
  Ex. 32. 1 ‖ Prov. 14. 17, 29 ‖ Ecclus. 20. 15.

102. *Of meekness.*
  Num. 12. 3 ‖ 1 Sam. 25. 20 ‖ 2 Sam. 22. 36 ‖ Ps. 25. 8 | 34. 2 | 37. 11 | 45. 5 *m* | 76. 9 | 86. 5

147. 6 | 149. 4 ‖ Prov. 3. 31 | 12. 10 ‖ Is. 11. 4
40. 7 ‖ Jer. 11. 19 ‖ Zeph. 2. 3 ‖ Ecclus. 5. 11
10. 28 ‖ S. Matt. 5. 5 | 11. 29 ‖ S. James 1. 21 *l.*

103. *Of patience.*
2 Sam. 16. 10 ‖ Job 5. 17 | 7. 1 | 13. 15 | 41. 8
Prov. 14. 29 | 15. 1 | 16. 32 | 19. 11 | 25. 15
Wis. 3. 5 ‖ Ecclus. 1. 23 | 2. 4, 14 | 6. 5 | Bar. 4. 25
1. Macc. 8. 4 ‖ 2. Macc. 6. 30 | 7. 36 ‖ S. Matt. 5. 9
10. 22 | 18. 26 ‖ S. Luke 6. 28, 29 | 21. 19
S. John 16. 20 ‖ Acts. 14. 22 *l* ‖ Rom. 5. 3 | 8. 18. 25
15. 4 ‖ 1 Cor. 13. 4 ‖ 2 Cor. 6. 4 | 12. 9 Gal. 5. 22
2 Tim. 2. 3 | 3. 12 ‖ Heb. 10. 36 | 12. 1 ‖ S. James 1. 12
5. 7, 8 | 1 S. Pet. 2. 19 | 3. 14 ‖ Rev. 2. 7 | 3. 21
13. 10 *l* | 14. 12 *f.*

104. *Against envy in general.*
Gen. 4. 5 | 26. 14 | 37. 8, 11, 20 ‖ 1 Sam. 3. 2, 3
18. 9 ‖ Job 5. 2, 14 ‖ Ps. 78. 46 ‖ Prov. 14. 30
Wis. 2. 24 | 6. 23 | 7. 13 ‖ S. Matt. 7. 1 | 20. 15
S. Luke 7. 49 ‖ S. John 12. 5 ‖ Gal. 5. 15, 21 *f*
S. James 3. 14 | 4. 5 ‖ 1 S. Pet. 2. 1.

105. *Against those who rejoice in the misfortunes of others.*
1 Sam. 15. 35 ‖ 2 Sam. 1. 20, 24 | 16. 7
Job 31. 29 ‖ Ps. 3. 1 | 79. 4 ‖ Prov. 14. 21 | 17. 5 *l*
24. 17 ‖ Is. 14. 10 | 22. 3 ‖ Jer. 38. 19 | 48. 26
Lam. 1. 21 *m* | 2. 15 | 3. 14 ‖ Ezek. 25. 3 ‖ Mic. 7. 8
2 Cor. 11. 29 ‖ Rev. 11. 10.

106. *Against hatred.*
Gen. 4. 5 | 27. 41 | 31. 5 | 34. 25 | 37. 4 | 49. 7
Ex. 1. 12 *l* | 20. 13 | 21. 12 ‖ Lev. 3. 3 | 19. 17 *f*
Num. 35. 18 ‖ Deut. 19. 11 ‖ 1 Sam. 24. 5 | 26. 8
Job 31. 29 ‖ Prov. 20. 22 | 25. 21 | 26. 26 | Ecclus. 9. 6
Jer. 15. 1 ‖ Ezek. 25. 12, 15 ‖ Amos 1. 2
Ecclus. 8. 7 | 10. 6 ‖ S. Luke 6. 32 | 23. 34
S. John 15. 8 ‖ Acts 7. 59 ‖ Rom. 12. 17
1 S. John 2. 9 | 4. 20.

107. *Against discord.*
    Ps. 133. 1 ‖ Prov. 6. 14, 19 *l* | 15. 18
    Ecclus. 27. 14, 15 | 28. 11 ‖ S. Matt. 12. 25
    1 Cor. 7. 15 *l* | 14. 33 ‖ Gal. 5. 20 *l*.

108. *Against an evil solitude.*
    Gen. 39. 11 *l* ‖ Eccles. 4. 10 ‖ Jer. 49. 31
    Lam. 1. 1 *f* ‖ 1 Cor. 9. 22.

109. *Against those that return evil for good.*
    Deut. 32. 6 ‖ Judg. 9. 16 | 2 Sam. 10. 4 | 11. 15
    2 Chron. 24. 22 | Ps. 35. 12 | 38. 20 | 109. 4
    Joel 3. 4 ‖ Ecclus. 29. 6 ‖ 1 Macc. 16. 17
    S. John 10. 32.

110. *Against those that return evil for evil; or against revenge.*
    Lev. 19. 18 | 1 Sam 12. 23 ‖ 2 Sam. 16. 10
    Ezek. 25. 12 | Ecclus. 10. 6 | 28. 1 ‖ S. Matt. 5. 44
    6. 15 | 18. 21 | S. Luke 23. 34 ‖ Rom. 12. 14, 17.

111. *Against murder.*
    Gen. 4. 10 ‖ Ex. 20. 13 | 21. 12 ‖ Lev. 24. 17
    Num. 35. 16 | Deut. 5. 17 | 19. 11 ‖ Ps. 5. 6 *l*
    55. 25 *f* | 79. 3 ‖ Prov. 6. 17 ‖ Is. 1. 15 | 59. 3
    Ezek. 18. 10 | 22. 12 *f* | 24. 6 ‖ S. Matt. 23. 35
    26. 52 ‖ Gal. 5. 21 | 1 S. John 3. 15 ‖ Rev. 13. 10
    21. 8.

112. *Of those who are punished with the instrument of their own sin.*
    1 Sam. 17. 51 | Esth. 7. 10 | Ps. 7. 16 | 9. 15
    35. 8 | 57. 6 | Prov. 26. 27 | 28. 10 | Is. 33. 1
    Judith 13. 6 ‖ S. Matt. 7. 2 ‖ S. Luke 6. 38
    Gal. 6. 7 ‖ Rev. 18. 6.

113. *Against those who unite in doing evil: or, that make a conspiracy against others.*
    Gen. 14. 1 | 34. 25 | 37. 18 ‖ Ex. 32. 2 ‖ Num. 16. 1
    2 Sam. 15. 12 *l* | Prov. 1. 10 ‖ Is. 1. 23 | 8. 12
    Jer. 11. 19 | 38. 5 | Dan. 6. 4 ‖ Wis. 2. 10
    S. John 11. 47 ‖ Gal. 5. 20.

114. *Of congratulation.*
Gen. 43. 30 | 45. 1, 15, 26 | 46. 29 || Tob. 11. 13
13. 14 || S. Luke 15. 6, 32 || S. John 20. 20
Acts 12. 14 || Rom. 12. 15 || 1 Cor. 13. 6 *l*.

115. *That we must love our enemies.*
Ex. 23. 4 || Prov. 25. 21 || S. Matt. 5. 44
S. Luke 6. 27 || Rom. 12. 20.

116. *Of unity and concord, and their fruits.*
Gen. 6. 14. 16 | 45. 24 || 1 Sam. 1. 6 | 6. 12
Ps. 22. 20 | 26. 11 | 27. 4 | 68. 6 | 133. 1 || Cant. 6. 9
Is. 8. 9 | 45. 20 || Judith 15. 5 *f* | S. Matt. 18. 19
S. Luke 10. 42 || Acts 4. 32 || Rom. 15. 6
1 Cor. 9. 24 Eph. 4. 3 || 1 S. Peter. 3. 8 || Rev. 19. 17.

117. *That we are to keep peace with all; or of those that pacify tumults.*
Gen. 13. 8 | 45. 24 || Num. 13. 30 || Judg. 8. 2, 3
Ps. 122. 7 | Is. 32. 17 | 52. 7 || Zech. 8. 19 *l*
S. Matt. 5. 9 || S. Mark. 9. 50 || S. Luke 10. 5
24. 35 | S. John 14. 27 | Rom. 12. 18 | 14. 19
Gal. 5. 26 | Philip. 4. 7 | Col. 3. 13 || 1 Thess. 5.
13 *l*, 26 || Heb. 12. 14 | 13. 20.

118. *Of reconciliation.*
Gen. 33. 10 | 40. 21 | 50. 17 2 Sam. 14. 21
Ecclus. 22. 21 | 1 Macc. 10. 26, 54 || S. Matt. 5. 23
S. Luke 23. 12 | Eph. 2. 16 | S. James 5. 20.

119. *Against idleness or listlessness, and their effects.*
Want—Prov. 10. 4 | 13. 4 | 14. 4 | 18. 9 | 19. 15
20. 4 | 21. 5, 25 | 28. 19 || Eccles. 10. 18.
Anguish—Prov. 15. 19.
It dissipates—Prov. 24. 31.
It is hateful to God—S. Matt. 25. 26 || S. Luke 19. 22.
It is conceited—Prov. 26. 16.

It deprives of good things—S. Matt. 25. 28
S. Luke 19. 24.
It remains in the same condition—Prov. 26. 14.
It is timid—Prov. 26. 13.
It is accursed—Jer. 48. 10.

120. *Against idleness in general.*
Gen. 3. 19 | Ex. 17. 11 || Num. 21. 4 *l* || Josh. 18. 3
Judg. 18. 9 *l* | Ps. 73. 5, 6 | 128. 2 || Prov. 6. 6
12. 24 | 16. 26 | 22. 29 | 31. 19 || Eccles. 5. 12
9. 4, 10 | 11. 6 | Is. 35. 3 | Zech. 8. 9 || Ecclus. 2. 2
6. 26 | 7. 15 *f* | 40. 30 || S. Matt. 20. 6 | 23. 3
25. 24 || S. Luke 19. 20 | S. John 5. 8 | Rom. 13. 11
Gal. 6. 9 | Eph. 5. 14 | Philip. 3. 13 || Col. 4. 17
2 Thess. 3. 8 | 2 Tim. 4. 5 || Heb. 12. 12.

121. *Against the sorrows of this world.*
Prov. 12. 21 | 15. 13 | 17. 22 | 25. 20 | Ecclus.
25. 13 *f* | 30. 22, 25 | 38. 20 | S. Mark 10. 22
S. Luke 18. 23 | 2 Cor. 7. 10.

122. *That we are not to lament the dead, or the calamities of this life beyond measure.*
2 Sam. 12. 20 | Job 1. 21 | 2. 10 || Jon. 4. 9.
1 Thess. 4. 13.

123. *That we must be watchful; or against an evil security, because the day of the* LORD *will come like a thief.*
Judg. 4. 21 | 16. 3, 19 | 18. 7 || Ps. 77. 6 | 119. 147
Prov. 4. 23 | 6. 9 | 8. 17 *l* | 21. 13 | Eccles. 7. 14
9. 12 | Jer. 48. 11 | 49. 31 | Wis. 6. 14 | Ecclus. 5. 1
11. 19 | 39. 5 || S. Matt. 24. 42 | 25. 13 | S. Mark 13. 33
14. 13 || S. Luke 12. 19 | 17. 24 | 21. 26 || Rom. 13. 11
1 Cor. 11. 30 | 15. 34 || Col. 4. 2 || 1 Thess. 5. 2
1 Tim. 6. 20 || 2 Tim. 4. 5 || 1 S. Pet. 4. 7 || Rev. 3. 2
16. 15.

124. *Against vain dreams.*
Is. 29. 8 | Eccles. 5. 7 | Ecclus. 34. 2.

(59)

125. *Of time and its loss.*
Deut. 32. 35 ‖ Job 7. 3 ‖ Ps. 145. 15 *l* ‖ Eccles. 3. 1
7. 17 *l* | 8. 6 | 9. 12 ‖ Is. 13. 22 *l.* ‖ Jer. 8. 7
Ezek. 7. 12 ‖ Hag. 1. 2 ‖ Ecclus. 4. 23 ‖ 1 Macc. 12. 1
2 Macc. 6. 25 ‖ S. Mark 13. 33 ‖ S. Luke 19. 44
S. John 12. 35 ‖ Rom. 13. 11 ‖ 2 Cor. 6. 2
Gal. 6. 10 ‖ Eph. 5. 16 | 6. 18 ‖ Heb. 5. 12
1 S. Pet. 4. 17.

126. *Against those that are negligent.*
1 Sam. 3. 13 ‖ 1 Kings 20. 32 ‖ 2 Kings 12. 7
22. 5 ‖ 2 Chron. 24. 6 ‖ Prov. 1. 25 ‖ Jer. 48. 10.

127. *Against omissions and venial sins; or, against those who neglect small things.*
Ecclus. 19. 1 *l* ‖ S. Matt. 25. 35, 36.

128. *Of spiritual joy; or of doing good works with gladness.*
Ex. 15. 1, 20 ‖ Judg. 5. 1 ‖ 1 Sam. 2. 1 ‖ 2 Sam. 5. 3
Neh. 8. 10 ‖ Job 31. 17 ‖ Ps. 19. 5 *l* | 118. 24
Prov. 16. 15 | 17. 22. ‖ Eccles. 9. 8 ‖ Is. 30. 29
51. 3 | 52. 1, 9 | 54. 1 | 60. 5 | 65. 14 ‖ Jer. 31. 21
Zech. 10. 7 ‖ Ecclus. 4. 2 | 18. 15 | 30. 23, 25
31. 28 | 35. 10 | 45. 23 ‖ S. Matt. 6. 16 ‖ 2 Cor. 9. 7
12. 9.

129. *Of the fervour of progress, and the anxiety to accomplish all duties.*
1 Sam. 25. 18 ‖ Ps. 5. 3 ‖ Prov. 8. 17 | 10. 4
12. 24 | 22. 6. 29 | 27. 1 ‖ Eccles. 9. 10 | 11. 6
Cant. 7. 12 ‖ Is. 35. 2 ‖ Lam. 3. 27 ‖ Zeph. 2. 14
Zech. 8. 9 ‖ Ecclus. 5. 7 | 6. 18 | 14. 13 | 25. 3
51. 20, 30 ‖ Heb. 4. 11 | 12. 12 ‖ Rev. 3. 15.

130. *That we must always advance in goodness.*
Gen. 9. 1 | 26. 12 | 28. 14 | 35. 11 ‖ Job 5. 25
8. 7 | 11. 17 | 29. 20 | 39. 26 | 42. 10 *l* ‖ Ps. 1. 3
84. 7 ‖ Prov. 4. 18 | 11. 28 *l* ‖ Is. 37. 31 ‖ Ecclus. 18. 7
Bar. 4. 28 ‖ S. Luke 17. 7 ‖ S. John 15. 2
1 Cor. 9. 24 ‖ 2 Cor. 9. 10 ‖ Philip. 1. 6 | 3. 12
2 S. Pet. 1. 5, 12.

131. *That we must always ascend.*
Gen. 13. 1 | 22. 12 | 45. 25 | 46. 31 ‖ Ex. 19. 13 *l*, 24 *m* | 24. 12 ‖ Judg. 1. 4 | 2. 1 | 13. 30 ‖ 1 Sam. 1. 3 *f* 23. 29 ‖ 2 Kings 2. 11 | 16. 5 ‖ 1 Chron. 21. 19 Ps. 24. 3 | 47. 5 ‖ Cant. 3. 6 | 7. 8.

132. *That counsels are to be added to commands.*
Job 1. 8 ‖ Is. 2. 3 | 54. 2 ‖ Jer. 31. 38.

(61)

Third Part.

133. *Of the sins of the tongue.*
   Prov. 13. 3 ‖ 15. 2 | 18. 6, 21 | 26. 9 | 29. 11
   Ecclus. 25. 15 ‖ S. James 3. 5.

134. *Against a boasting tongue.*
   Judg. 12. 5 ‖ 1 Sam. 3. 19 ‖ Job 11. 2 | 13. 5
   19. 2 | 32. 19, 20 | 38. 2 ‖ Prov. 5. 1 | 9. 13
   10. 19 | 14. 23 | 15. 2 | 16. 28 | 17. 14, 27 | 18. 7, 21
   23. 9 | 25. 11 | 26. 7 | 29. 11 Eccles. 5. 1, 6 *f*
   10. 13 ‖ Is. 11. 25 | 29. 4 ‖ Ecclus. 4. 29 | 5. 14
   7. 14 | 14. 1 | 19. 6, 16 | 20. 5, 13, 20 | 21. 25
   23. 15 | 25. 8 | 27. 7 | 28. 25 ‖ S. Matt. 12. 36
   26. 73 *l* ‖ S. Mark 14. 70 ‖ S. Luke 16. 24
   S. John 3. 31 *m* ‖ Eph. 5. 3 ‖ Col. 4. 6 ‖ 1 Tim. 6. 3
   2 Tim. 2. 14, 23 ‖ Tit. 3. 9 ‖ S. James 1. 19, 26
   3. 2 ‖ 1 S. John 4. 5.

135. *Against boasting.*
   Job 32. 10 | 33. 5, 31 ‖ Ps. 12. 4 | 73. 9
   Prov. 26. 23 | 27. 2 | 28. 25 ‖ Ezek. 28. 2
   Dan. 4. 30 | 7. 8 *l*.

136. *Of lying and false witness.*
   Gen. 3. 4 | 4. 9 ‖ Ex. 20. 16 Lev. 19. 11
   Deut. 5. 20 ‖ Job 13. 7 ‖ Ps. 5. 6, 10 | 18. 44
   27. 12 ‖ Eccles. 5. 4 ‖ Is. 59. 3, 13 *l* ‖ Jer. 9. 3 *f*, 5
   Hos. 4. 2 | 7. 1 *m*, 13 *l* | 10. 4 ‖ Nah. 3. 1
   Ecclus. 4. 25 | 7. 13 | 20. 18 | 34. 4 *l* ‖ Sus. 55.
   1 Macc. 13. 19 ‖ S. John 8. 44 Acts 5. 1, 8
   2 Cor. 1. 18 ‖ Col. 3. 9 ‖ Rev. 14. 5 | 21. 8 *m*.

137. *Against those that swear indiscreetly, and that perjure themselves.*
   Ex. 20. 7 ‖ Deut. 5. 11 ‖ Ps. 15. 5 ‖ Prov. 20. 25
   Ezek. 17. 46 ‖ Zech. 5. 3 *l* | Ecclus. 23. 9 | 27. 14
   S. Matt. 5. 33 ‖ S. James 5. 12.

138. *That an oath is sometimes lawful.*

Gen. 22. 16 | 24. 3 | 31. 53 *l* | 47. 31 ‖ Ex. 22. 11 1 Sam. 3. 14 ‖ Ps. 89. 3, 34 | 95. 11 | 110. 4 119. 106 | 132. 2 ‖ Jer. 40. 9 ‖ Dan. 12. 7 ‖ Amos 6. 8 S. Matt. 5. 33 | 23. 16, 18 ‖ S. Luke 1. 73 ‖ Rom. 1. 9 9. 1 ‖ 2 Cor. 1. 23 ‖ Gal. 1. 20 ‖ Heb. 3. 18 | 6. 13 Rev. 10. 6.

139. *That an oath is sometimes not lawful.*

Ex. 20. 7 ‖ S. Matt. 5. 34 ‖ S. James 5. 12.

140. *Against those who indiscreetly promise or vow.*

Lev. 6. 1—7 ‖ Num. 30 ‖ Deut. 23. 23 ‖ Ps. 61. 8 76. 11 ‖ Eccles. 5, 2 ‖ Jon. 2. 9 ‖ Ecclus. 4. 29 8. 13.

141. *Against detractors.*

Ex. 22. 28 ‖ Lev. 19. 14 ‖ Job 19. 18 ‖ Ps. 41. 7 50. 20 | 57. 5 | 69. 12 | 101. 6 | 109. 3 ‖ Prov. 4. 24 24. 9 *l* | 25. 23 | 30. 14 ‖ Eccles. 10. 11 ‖ Wis. 1. 11 Ecclus. 28. 15 ‖ S. James 4. 11.

142. *Against those that flatter others when present, and accuse them when absent.*

Ps. 10. 7 | 12. 2 | 57. 5 ‖ Prov. 10. 18 | 11. 9 14. 25 | 17. 20 | 18. 8 | 26. 22 ‖ Jer. 9. 8 Ecclus. 5. 14 | 27. 22 ‖ S. Luke 22. 48.

143. *Against whisperers and double-tongued men; and against those that sow discord.*

Lev. 19. 16 ‖ Ps. 41. 7 ‖ Prov. 6. 19 | 18. 8 26. 20 ‖ Ecclus. 5. 14 | 21. 28 | 28. 15 ‖ 1 Macc. 7. 6, 10 ‖ 2 Macc. 4. 46 | 14. 26.

144. *Against accusers.*

Gen. 37. 2 ‖ Prov. 25. 9.

145. *Against those who reveal secrets.*

Gen. 9. 22 ‖ Num. 19. 15 ‖ Prov. 11. 13 | 17. 9 25. 9 ‖ Tob. 12. 7 ‖ Ecclus. 19. 10 | 22. 27 27. 17, 21 *l* | 37. 7.

(63)

146. *Against those that are suspicious, and judge rashly.*
Job 4. 7 | 8. 13 | 11. 2. 14 | 15. 3 | 18. 4 | 20. 5
22. 15, 21 ‖ Ps. 119. 39 ‖ Jer. 17. 9 ‖ Wis. 17. 10
S. Matt. 7. 1 ‖ S. Luke 7. 33, 39 ‖ S. John 7. 24
8. 7, 52 ‖ Rom. 14. 1, 13 ‖ 1 Cor. 4. 3 ‖ S. James 4. 11.

147. *Against a tongue that seduces to sin.*
Job 2. 9 | 14. 5 ‖ Prov. 7. 21 | Is. 9. 51 *l* ‖ 1 Cor.
15. 33 ‖ Job 5. 7 ‖ Col. 2. 18 ‖ 2 Tim. 2. 16 ‖ Tit. 1. 10.

148. *Against those that murmur.*
Ex. 16. 2 ‖ Num. 11. 1 | 16. 41 | 20. 2 | 21. 5
Ps. 59. 15 ‖ Is. 45. 10 | 60. 4 ‖ Wis. 1. 10
S. John 6. 41 ‖ 1 Cor. 10. 19.

149. *Against those that murmur against the works of* GOD.
Job 5. 6 | 9. 12 | 11. 10 | 21. 5 ‖ Ps. 75. 6
Is. 10. 15 | 45. 9 ‖ Ecclus. 39. 33 ‖ Rom. 9. 20.

150. *Against blasphemy.*
Ex. 5. 2 ‖ Lev. 24. 16 ‖ Job 34. 37 ‖ Is. 1. 4
10. 15 | 45. 9 ‖ Ecclus. 39. 33 ‖ Rom. 9. 20.

151. *Against those that are contentious and quarrelsome.*
Job 19. 5 ‖ Prov. 14. 3 | 15. 1 | 16. 28 | 18. 6
19. 13 | 20. 3 | 26. 17 ‖ Gal. 5. 20.

152. *Against a clamorous and contentious tongue.*
Prov. 13. 10 | 17. 11, 23 | 24. 19 ‖ Ecclus. 8. 1 ‖ 1 Cor.
3. 3 ‖ Eph. 4. 31 ‖ Philip. 2. 3 ‖ 2 Tim. 2. 24 ‖ Tit. 3. 9.

153. *Against cursing.*
Gen. 12. 3 | 27. 29 ‖ Ex. 21. 17 ‖ Lev. 20. 9
Num. 23. 8 ‖ 1 Sam. 17. 43 ‖ 2 Sam. 16. 5 | 19. 21
Job 31. 30 ‖ Prov. 20. 20 | 26. 2 | 30. 11 ‖ S. John
9. 28 ‖ Rom. 12. 14 ‖ S. James. 3. 9.

154. *That all our words should be to edification.*
Deut 32. 2 | Ps. 37. 31 | 49. 3 ‖ Prov. 10. 31
11. 25 | 12. 17, 19 | 15. 1, 7 | 18. 4 | 25. 11 | 29. 11
Eccles. 3. 7 *l* | 9. 17 | 10. 12 ‖ Cant. 2. 14 | 4. 11
Mal. 2. 7 ‖ Ecclus. 6. 5 | 18. 16 | 20. 6, 13, 29
21. 16 | 22. 6 ‖ S. Matt. 12. 35 ‖ Eph. 4. 29
Col. 4. 6 ‖ 1 Thess. 5. 11.

155. *Of truth.*

Ps. 12. 3 | 45. 5 | 85. 11 | 89. 15, 25 ‖ Jer. 9. 5 Zech. 8. 16 ‖ S. John 8. 40 | 14. 6 | 17. 17 | 18. 37 *l* Rom. 3. 4.

156. *Of watchfulness over the tongue, and of silence.*

Ex. 14. 14 ‖ 1 Sam. 3. 19 ‖ Job 13. 5 ‖ Ps. 1. 3 39. 1 ‖ Prov. 10. 8 *l* | 13. 2 | 17. 38 | 18. 21 21. 23 | 23. 9 | 26. 4 ‖ Eccles. 5. 6 ‖ Is. 30. 15 *m* 32. 17 *l* | 53. 7 ‖ Lam. 3. 26 ‖ Zeph. 1. 7 Ecclus. 22. 27 | 27. 13 | 28. 25 | 32. 7, 9 *l* ‖ S. John 19. 9 ‖ Eph. 4. 29 ‖ S. James 1. 19.

157. *Against the sin of the eyes.*

Gen. 3. 6 | 34. 1 | 39. 7 ‖ Josh. 7. 21 ‖ 2 Sam. 11. 2 Job 24. 15 | 31. 1 ‖ Ps. 119. 37 ‖ Prov. 4. 25 17. 24 *l* | 23. 5 *f*, 31 | 30. 13 ‖ Is. 33. 15 *l* Lam. 3. 49 ‖ Ecclus. 9. 7 | 42. 12 ‖ S. Matt. 5. 28, 29.

158. *Against the sin of the ears.*

Gen. 3. 17. ‖ Ex. 6. 12 ‖ Deut. 18. 19 | 28. 15 1 Sam. 2. 25 *l* ‖ 1 Kings 20. 36. | 21. 12 ‖ Prov. 21. 13 28. 9 ‖ Is. 5. 12 | 33. 15 *l* ‖ Jer. 7. 24 ‖ Amos 6. 5 Zech. 7. 11 ‖ Mal. 2. 1.

159. *Against the sin of smelling.*

Is. 3. 24 *f* ‖ Ezek. 8. 17 *l*.

160. *Of the five senses, and keeping them from sin.*

Jos. 10. 17, 18 ‖ 2 Kings 9. 33 ‖ Neh. 7. 3 Job 39. 20 ‖ Prov. 13. 3 ‖ Is. 19. 16 | 60. 8 Jer. 9. 21 ‖ Joel 2. 9 ‖ Eccles. 21. 23 ‖ S. Mark 14. 5 2 Cor. 6. 17.

Fourth Part.

161. *Of the seven deadly sins.*
Gen. 15. 17 | 41. 3, 6 || Deut. 7. 1 || Prov. 6. 16 Bel. 32 || S. Matt. 12. 45 || S. Luke 8. 2 | 11. 26 Rev. 13. 1 | 15. 1 | 17. 3.

162. *Of the seven gifts of the* Holy Ghost.
Ex. 25. 37 || Is. 4. 1 | 11. 2 || Zech. 3. 9 | 4. 2

163. *Of the gifts or graces of* God.
Jer. 5. 24 || Wis. 2. 23 || Ecclus. 17. 1 | 38. 4 Acts 7. 10 | Rom. 12. 6 || 1 Cor. 12. 7, 28 | 14. 2, 39 Eph. 4. 11 || S. James 1. 17.

164. *Of the fourfold manifestation of sin.*
Gen. 14. 1 || Prov. 30. 21 || Dan. 7. 2, 3, 6 | 8. 8 Amos 1. 3 || S. John 11. 17 || Rev. 9. 14.

165. *Of the threefold army of the devil; or, the threefold manifestation of sin.*
Gen. 3. 5 || Ex. 5. 11, 12, 16 || Job. 1. 17 || Ps. 11. 7 Is. 28. 1 || Jer. 5. 6 || Ezek. 4. 3 || Hab. 2. 6 Ecclus. 25. 2 | 26. 28 || S. Matt. 4. 3, 6, 8 || S. Luke 4. 3, 5, 9 || 1 S. John 2. 16 || Rev. 8. 11, 13 | 9. 18.

166. *Of the threefold remedy against the threefold assaults of the devil.*
Ex. 3. 18 *l.* || Prov. 30. 29 || Is. 58. 9 || Joel 2. 12 *l* S. James 4. 7.

167. *Of the manifold setting forth of virtues.*
Gen. 2. 10 || Deut. 10. 17 || 1 Sam. 16. 18 || Job 4. 6 22. 23 | 30. 1 | Ps. 15. 1 || Prov. 1. 1 | 2. 5 | 3. 5 | 9. 1 30. 24, 29 | 31. 13 || Cant. 4. 13 || Is. 11. 1 | 58. 6, 9 Ezek. 18. 5 || Mic. 6. 8 || Mal. 2. 5 || Wis. 7. 22 | 8. 7 Ecclus. 25. 1 || 2 Macc. 15. 22 || S. Matt. 5. 3 | 25. 34 Rom. 5. 3 | 13. 7 || 1 Cor. 13. 4 | 16. 13 || 2 Cor. 6. 4 7. 11 || Gal. 5. 22 || Eph. 4. 1 | 6. 14 || Philip 4. 8 Col. 1. 19 | 3. 12 || 1 Thess. 5. 13 || 1 Tim. 3. 2 | 4. 12 6. 11 || 2 Tim. 2. 22 || Tit. 1. 7 | 2. 2, 12 | 3. 1 || Heb. 13. 1, 2 || S. James 3. 17 || 2 S. Pet. 1. 5.

F

(66)

168. *Of the manifold setting forth of vices.*
Ex. 20. 3 ǁ Lev. 19. 4 | 20. 2 ǁ Job 22. 6 | 24. 2
Ps. 12. 2 | 14. 1 ǁ Prov. 6. 12, 16 | 23. 29 | 30. 11, 15
Is. 1. 4, 21 | 3. 16 | 5. 8, 18 | 32. 6 | 59. 12 ǁ Jer. 7. 9
9. 4 ǁ Ezek. 16. 49 | 18. 10 | 34. 3 ǁ Hos. 4. 1
Mic. 3. 9 ǁ Wis. 2. 6 | 14. 23 ǁ Ecclus. 22. 2 | 25. 2
26. 5, 28 | 40. 20 ǁ S. Matt. 12. 45 | 15. 18 | 25. 42
Rom. 1. 29 | 2. 21 | 13. 9, 13 ǁ 1 Cor. 5. 10 | 6. 10
10. 7 | 2 Cor. 12. 20 ǁ Gal. 5. 19 ǁ Eph. 5. 3
Col. 3. 5 ǁ 1 Tim. 2. 9 ǁ 2 Tim. 3. 2 ǁ 1 S. Pet. 2. 1
4. 3, 15 ǁ S. Jude 8. 16 ǁ Rev. 21. 8.

169. *That we must cast out all vices; or, that we must put off the Old Man and put on the New Man.*
Gen. 15. 11 | 41. 14 ǁ Rev. 14. 8, 39 ǁ Deut. 20. 17
Josh. 11. 11 ; Judg: 6. 25 ǁ 2 Kings 23. 4, 19 ǁ Job 2. 7
11. 14 ǁ Ps. 78. 56 | 80. 9 ǁ Prov. 25. 4 ǁ Jer. 1. 10
4. 3 ǁ Ezek. 36. 26 ǁ Tob. 8. 3 ǁ 11. 11 | Judith 10. 3
1 Macc. 44. 3 | 14. 36 ǁ 2 Macc. 3. 3 | 12. 38
S. Mark 3. 15 ǁ S. Luke 8. 2, 29 | 11. 14 | 23. 52
Acts 9. 18 ǁ Rom. 12. 2 | 13. 12 ǁ 1 Cor. 5. 7
2 Cor. 4. 16 ǁ Eph. 4. 22 ǁ Heb. 12. 1.

BOOK II.

First Part.

170. *That we ought to be anxious for the salvation of others.*

Gen. 4. 9 *f* | 35. 2 ‖ Ex. 26. 3 ‖ Ps. 34. 3, 11
51. 13 | 95. 1 ‖ Prov. 5. 16 | 24. 11 ‖ Is. 2. 3
30. 20 | 31. 6 ‖ Jer. 15, 19 *l* | 16. 16 ‖ Ecclus. 33. 17
S. Mark 5. 19 ‖ S. Luke 8. 39 ‖ S. John 1. 41, 45
4. 28 ‖ 1 Tim. 4. 13, 16 ‖ S. James 5. 19, 20
1 S. Pet. 5. 2 ‖ Rev. 22. 17.

171. *Of conversion from the world and from sin.*

Gen. 4. 7 | 19. 14 | 21. 8 | 28. 19 | 29. 1 | 49. 6, 21 *f*
Ex. 3. 8 | 9. 1 | 10. 29 | 16. 6 ‖ 2 Chron. 30. 8 | 34. 3
Job 36. 10, 20 ‖ Ps. 1. 1 ‖ Prov. 3. 28 ‖ Is. 30. 21
43. 25 | 44. 22 | 45. 22 | 46. 8 | 49. 9 ‖ Jer. 4. 1
7. 13 | 8. 6 | 18. 8 | 25. 5 Ezek. 18. 30 | 33. 11
Joel 2. 12 ‖ Zeph. 2. 3 ‖ Haggai 1. 2 ‖ Mal. 3. 7 *l*
Ecclus. 5. 7 ‖ S. Matt. 3. 2 | 11. 28 | 19. 29 | 22. 4
S. Mark 11. 13 ‖ Rev. 22. 17.

172. *That we ought to stir up others to repentance and conversion.*

Gen. 41. 14 ‖ Ex. 12. 15 | 13. 3 | 15. 22 *f*
Ruth 3. 1 ‖ 1 Sam. 7. 3 ‖ Cant. 3. 11 ‖ Is. 1. 16
30. 15 | 45. 22 | 48. 20 ‖ Jer. 3. 1 *l*, 12 | 6. 26
8. 14 | 13. 16, 18 | 31. 21 | 47. 19 | 50. 8 ‖ Lam.
3. 40 ‖ Hos. 2. 14 | 6. 1 | 12. 13 *f* ‖ Jon. 2. 6
Wis. 10. 1.

173. *That enormous sinners, when converted, may be profitable to others by their teaching and example.*

Job 28. 2 ‖ Ps. 68. 22 ‖ Prov. 27. 27 | 31. 14
Is. 17. 2 | 35. 7 | 43. 6 | 55. 13 | 60. 4 *l* ‖ Jer. 30. 10 *m*
51. 48 ‖ Hos. 1. 2 *m* | 2. 15 ‖ S. Matt. 4. 17
Rom. 5. 20 *l*.

174. *That conversion is hearty in thought and in deed, if we renounce the details of sin.*

Gen. 14. 3 | 19. 17 *m* | 35. 2 | 45. 20 ‖ Ex. 10. 26
12. 15 *f* ‖ Lev. 12. 8 ‖ Deut. 7. 2, 25 *m* | 12. 3
Josh. 12. 28 | 23. 12 ‖ Judg. 6. 20 | 1 Sam. 15. 18
Job 11. 14 ‖ Ps. 45. 11 *l* ‖ Prov. 5. 8 ‖ Jer. 4. 1
50. 8 ‖ Hos. 2. 17 ‖ Ecclus. 21. 2 ‖ Eph. 5. 3.

175. *That repentance should be taken in hand speedily for seven reasons.*

The first reason is, lest sin become a habit, which it is almost impossible to give up.

Jer. 8. 6 *l* | 9. 5 *l* | 12. 23 ‖ S. John 11. 39 *l*.

The second reason is, lest we should fall from one wickedness into another.

Ps. 42. 9 *f* ‖ Hos. 4. 2 ‖ Rom. 2. 5 ‖ Rev. 22. 11.

The third reason is, sudden death.

Prov. 27. 1 ‖ Eccles. 9. 15 ‖ S. Matt. 25. 13
S. Luke 12. 20, 40 ‖ Rev. 3. 3 *l* | 16. 15 *l*.

The fourth reason is, that a man in his last sickness may be taken up by other matters, or may be slain by some unexpected accident.

1 Sam. 4. 18 | 31. 2 *l* ‖ 2 Sam. 20. 10 ‖ Eccles.
12. 1 ‖ Is. 38. 19 *f* ‖ Jer. 50. 24 | 51. 34.

The fifth reason is, lest man should be tormented by the pains of hell.
Job 20. 18 || 1 Cor. 3. 13 || Heb. 10. 31.

The sixth reason is, the difficulty of true repentance.
Job 18. 18 || Lam. 3. 53 *l* || Hos. 13. 12 || Zech. 5. 7

The seventh reason is, the shame which men feel in confessing the circumstances of their sins.
Cant. 1. 13 || Jer. 3. 3 *l* || S. Luke 18. 13 || Rom. 6. 21.

176. *Against those who put off confession or conversion.*
Gen. 19. 15 | 28. 18 || Prov. 3. 28 || Eccles. 12. 1 Wis. 6. 14 | 16. 27 || Lam. 3. 27 || Mic. 7. 1 Zeph. 2. 14 || Ecclus. 5. 4 | 5. 7 | 6. 18 | 25. 3 S. Matt. 21. 19 || S. Luke 13. 6.

177. *That evil and impenitent men die before the time which* God *had otherwise appointed for them.*
Gen. 20. 7 || Job 22. 16, 17 || Ps. 55. 25 | 78. 33 Prov. 10. 27 *l*.

178. *To the newly-converted.*
Deut. 21. 12 || Jer. 4. 3 | 7. 29 || Ezek. 5. 1 Ecclus. 2. 1.

179. *That those who are newly-converted are to be gently treated.*
Gen. 33. 13 || Is. 66. 13 || S. John 12. 2 || 1 Cor. 3. 2 Gal. 6. 1 || 1 Thess. 5. 14 || 2 Thess. 3. 15.

180. *That we are not to presume at the beginning of our conversion.*
Lev. 12. 4 *l* | 19. 23 || Ruth 2. 10 || 2. Sam. 10, 5 14. 33 || Job 4. 18 | 9. 15. 20, 30 || Jer. 3. 12 Dan. 9. 18 *l* || Ecclus. 5. 5 || S. Luke 7. 38 | 10. 39 15. 19 | 18. 13.

(70)

Second Part.

181. *Concerning the bitterness of contrition, and blaming ourselves.*

2 Sam. 24. 17 ‖ 1 Chron. 21. 8, 17 ‖ Ezra 9. 3
Neh. 1. 4 ‖ Job 9. 20 | 10. 1 *l* | 33. 27 | 42. 6
Ps. 6. 7 | 51. 17 | 147. 3 ‖ Is. 6. 5 | 38. 15 *l*
57. 15 *l* ‖ Mic. 7. 8 *f* ‖ S. Luke 15. 18 ‖ 1 Tim. 1. 15.

182. *That we ought abundantly to weep for our sins.*

Gen. 29. 11 | 37. 34 | 43. 30 ‖ Ex. 33. 4
Lev. 10. 6 *l* ‖ Num. 20. 29 ‖ Deut. 30. 1 ‖ Josh. 7. 5 *l*
Judg. 11. 35 ‖ Ruth 1. 9 *l* ‖ 1 Sam. 1. 7
1 Chron. 21. 16 ‖ Ezra 10. 1 ‖ Esth. 4. 1 ‖ Job 16. 15
Ps. 42. 3 | 119. 136 ‖ Prov. 13. 14 ‖ Eccles. 4. 1 *m*
7. 2 ‖ Cant. 1. 13 ‖ Is. 16. 9 | 22, 12 | 38. 3 *l*
59. 11 ‖ Jer. 6. 26 | 9. 1, 18 | 31. 9 *f* ‖ Lam. 2. 19 *f*
Ezek. 16. 61 ‖ Dan. 10. 2 ‖ Joel 2. 17 ‖ Jon. 3. 6
Wis. 3. 2 *l* ‖ Tob. 2. 5 ‖ Judith 8. 17 ‖ Ecclus.
7. 34 | 38. 19 ‖ Bar. 2. 18 ‖ 2 Macc. 3. 19
S. Matt. 5. 4 ‖ Luke 19. 41 ‖ Acts 20. 37
Philip. 3. 17 ‖ S. James 4. 9 ‖ Rev. 5. 4.

183. *That even the righteous man stands in need of repentance.*

Gen. 27. 16 ‖ Num. 19. 9 ‖ Job 25. 5 ‖ Is. 13. 10 *l*
50. 3 ‖ Jer. 31. 4 ‖ Ezek. 32. 7 ‖ Amos. 9. 6 ‖ Mal. 3. 3
Ecclus. 18. 6, 7 ‖ S. Luke 17. 10 ‖ S. John 15. 2 *l*
1 Cor. 9. 27.

184. *Of penitence, and the arms of penitence: or the armour of* God.

Gen. 2. 11 *l* ‖ Ex. 12. 11 | 28. 2 ‖ Deut. 30. 1
2 Sam. 12. 13 ‖ Ezra 10. 1 ‖ Neh. 8. 9 *l* ‖ Ps. 45. 4
Cant. 3. 7 ‖ Is. 38. 15 | 59. 17 | 61. 3 ‖ Jer. 4. 1
31. 21 *l* ‖ Ez. 30. 9 | 33. 11 ‖ Dan. 9. 3 ‖ Joel 2. 13
Jon. 3. 4 ‖ Bar. 4. 28 ‖ S. Matt. 3. 7 | 12. 41
S. Luke 18. 13 ‖ Eph. 6. 11 ‖ Col. 3. 12 ‖ Rev. 2. 5.

185. *Of the waters that flow down from mountains; that is, of holy doctrine, contrition, and baptism.*

Gen. 2. 10 | 26. 32 || Job 12. 15 || Ps. 65. 10, 11 72. 6 | 74. 14 | 104. 13 || Prov. 5. 15 || Cant. 5. 12 Is. 12. 3 | 55. 1 *f* || Jer. 2. 13 || Ezek. 17. 8 | 34. 26 *l* 47. 8 || Zech. 13. 1 | 14. 8 || S. John 2. 7 | 4. 14 Heb. 6. 7.

186. *That the rite of confession is to be prudently administered.*

Ex. 21. 33 || Num. 19. 15 || Ps. 81. 6 || Prov. 25. 9 *l* Haggai 2. 11 || Tob. 12. 7 || S. Matt. 23. 4 | 24. 35 S. Luke 10. 34.

187. *That the burden imposed is not to be out of proportion to the strength.*

Ex. 22. 24 || S. Matt. 9. 16 || S. Mark 2. 22 S. Luke 14. 28 || Rom. 12. 1 *l*.

188. *What confession ought to be.*

'Tis simple, humble, frequent, pure, sincere;
Open, discreet, free, modest, without fear;
'Tis perfect, secret, tearful, undelayed;
Brave, self-accusing, with obedience paid;
'Tis full of hope, or no fruit comes; addressed
To One that feels—the wisest and the best.
'Tis simple—Is. 20. 2 || Ecclus. 4. 26.
Humble—Ps. 51. 3.
Frequent—Neh. 9. 3 *l* || Is. 23. 16.
Pure—Ex. 12. 8 *l*.
Sincere—Job. 22. 2, 5.
Open—S. John 12. 3 *l*.
Discreet—Lev. 2. 13 || Rom. 12. 1.
Free—Ps. 54. 6.
Modest—Ezra 9. 6 || S. Luke 18. 13.
Without—fear—Ps. 130. 4.
'Tis perfect—Ps. 51. 9 || S. Matt. 18. 34 || S. James 2. 10.

Secret—Ps. 19. 12.
Tearful—1 Kings 21. 27 ‖ Neh. 1. 4 ‖ Is. 38. 3 *l*
Jon. 3. 6 ‖ S. Matt. 26. 75 ‖ S. Luke 7. 38.
Undelayed—Ecclus. 5. 7 ‖ S. Matt 5. 25.
Brave—2 Cor. 4. 16.
Self accusing—Job 7. 11 | 33. 27 ‖ Prov. 18. 17
S. Luke 15. 18
With obedience paid—Prov. 26. 11 ‖ Eccles. 12. 7
2 S. Pet 2. 21.
'Tis full of hope, or no fruit comes—Gen. 4. 13
S. Matt. 27. 3.
Addressed to one that feels—Ecclus. 12. 13.
The wisest—S. Luke 6. 39.
And the best—Jer. 5. 5 | 23. 28.

189. *Of confession and its fruit.*
Gen. 44. 18 ‖ Josh. 7. 19 ‖ Judg. 2. 18 *l* ‖ 10. 15
2 Sam. 14. 26 | 24. 10 *l* ‖ 2 Chron. 13. 18 ‖ Ezra 9. 6
Neh. 9. 3 *l* ‖ Job 7. 11 | 31. 33 | 33. 27 ‖ Ps. 32. 5
38. 4, 18 | 106. 6 ‖ Prov. 28. 13 ‖ Is. 64. 6 ‖ Jer. 3. 13
8. 6 ‖ Lam. 2. 19 *f* | 5. 15 ‖ Ez. 18. 30 *l* ‖ S. Matt. 3. 6
S. Luke 15. 7, 17 ‖ Acts 19. 18 ‖ 1 Cor. 11. 31
S. James 3. 17 *f* | 5. 16.

190. *Of satisfaction in this life.*
Gen. 37. 33 ‖ Josh. 7. 6 ‖ 2 Sam. 12 ‖ 1 Kings
21. 27 ‖ Ezra 9. 4 | 10. 1 ‖ Esth. 4. 16 ‖ Job 1. 20
16. 16 ‖ Is. 37. 1 ‖ Jer. 4. 8 | 9. 1 | 18. 8 ‖ Dan.
4. 27 | 9. 3 ‖ Joel 1. 13 ‖ Jon. 3. 5 ‖ Judith 4. 11
8. 5, 17 ‖ Bar. 4. 28 ‖ 2 Macc. 10. 25 ‖ S. Matt. 3. 2
12. 41 ‖ S. Luke 19. 8 ‖ Rom. 6. 19.

191. *As the righteousness of the righteous is well pleasing to* God, *so is the penitence of sinners; and that as much as we have given up ourselves to sin, so much we ought to return to* God.
Lev. 6. 25 | 7. 2 ‖ Is. 31. 6 ‖ Bar. 4. 28 ‖ S. Luke
7. 38 | 15. 7 | Rom. 5. 20 *l* | 6. 19.

192. *Of these three, contrition, confession, and satisfaction taken together.*

Gen. 22. 4 ‖ Ex. 3. 18 | 8. 27 ‖ Josh. 1. 11 | 7. 6 Judg. 1. 3 ‖ Cant. 4. 8 ‖ Is. 16. 14, 23 ‖ Jer. 31. 4 Dan. 5. 21 ‖ Hos. 2. 3 ‖ 1 Macc. 2. 66 ‖ S. Matt. 1. 3 ‖ S. Mark 10. 35 | 13. 33 ‖ Rom. 10. 10.

BOOK III.

First Part.

193. *Of those that return to* GOD, *or desire to return; and that after grace bestowed, the devil is wont to assault us grievously.*

Gen. 14. 17 | 26. 14 | 31. 22 | 37. 4 | Ex. 1. 9
5. 8 | 9. 31 ‖ 14. 5 ‖ 17. 8 ⁞ Josh. 10. 3, 4 ‖ 1 Sam.
7. 10 *f* ‖ 1 Kings 19. 1 ‖ Ezra 4. 1 ‖ Job 3. 8
7. 18 | 40. 23 ⁞ Ps. 3. 1 ‖ Is. 54. 11 | 59. 15
Hab. 1. 10 ⁞ Tob. 6. 2 ⁞ Jud. 1. 11 | 11. 1 | Ecclus.
2. 1 ⁞ 1 Macc. 5. 1 ⁞ S. Matt. 4. 1 | 8. 28 | S. Mark
9. 25 ‖ Acts 20. 9 *l* | 28. 3.

194. *Of the first motions to sin.*

Deut. 7. 2 ‖ Josh. 17. 13 | 23. 12 ‖ Judg. 1. 21
3. 1 ‖ Ps. 19. 13 | 29. 7 ⁞ Prov. 1. 10 ‖ Cant. 2. 15
Is. 52. 1 *l* ‖ Ecclus. 18. 30 ⁞ Rom. 8. 13 | 13. 14
1 Cor. 9. 27 *f* | Gal. 5. 24 ‖ S. James 4. 7 *l*
1 S. Pet. 2. 11.

195. *Of temptation.*

Gen. 22. 1 | 39. 9 ‖ Deut. 9. 22 | 13. 1 ‖ Job. 1. 11
2. 4 | 5. 19 ⁞ Judith 8. 12 ‖ Ecclus. 34. 10 ⁞ 1. Macc.
2. 52 ⁞ S. Matt. 4. 1 | 7. 25 | 14. 30 ⁞ S. Mark 1. 13
4. 37 | 10. 2 ‖ S. Luke 4. 2. | 8. 28 | 10. 20 ‖ 1 Cor.
10. 9, 13 ‖ S. James 1. 2, 13 | 4. 7 *l* ‖ 1 S. Pet. 5. 8.

196. *Against those that tempt* GOD.

Ex. 17. 7 ⁞ Deut. 6. 16 ‖ Judith 8. 12 ‖ S. Matt.
4. 7.

197. *Of the perseverance of the devil.*

Job 38. 30 ‖ Ecclus. 27. 10 | 48. 18 ‖ 2. Cor. 11. 14.
1 S. Pet. 5. 8.

198. *That the power of the devil is small if a man resist.*

Gen. 31. 24 || Job. 1. 10 || Is. 51. 23 || Ecclus. 10. 4 S, Matt. 4. 6 || S. Mark 5, 12 || S James 4. 7 S. John 5. 4.

199. *That the devil is always desirous of rejecting heavenly, and keeping earthly, things.*

Gen. 14. 13 || 1 Sam. 11. 2 || Prov. 17. 24 Eccles. 2. 14 || Jer. 4. 22 *l* || Zech. 11. 17 *l* || S. Luke 23. 18.

200. *That the devil is cruel, and his ways are hard.*

Deut. 6. 21 || Judg. 2. 19 || Ps. 38. 4 | Prov. 5. 9 15. 19 *f* || Is. 19. 4 | Jer. 2. 19 *m* | 9. 5 *l* | 16. 13 *l* Lam. 5. 5 || Hos. 12. 14 || Wis. 5. 7 *f* || Ecclus. 21. 10 || Acts 8. 23.

201. *That the way of the* LORD *is narrow at the beginning, but in the end, broad and pleasant.*

Ex. 25. 31 || Job 6. 7 || Ps. 119. 32, 103 || Prov. 3. 17 | 4. 11 | 8. 31 *l* | 15. 19 || Cant. 5. 1 || Is. 51. 3 58. 14 | 61. 1 *l* || Wis. 8. 1, 16 | 10. 10 || S. Matt. 11. 28 || S. Luke 13. 24 || S. John 2. 10.

202. *That men are sold to the devil on account of their sins.*

Is. 44. 22 *l* | 52. 3 || Rom. 6. 12 | 7. 14 *l* || 1 S. Pet. 1. 18.

203. *Of the devil and his fall.*

Job 1. 6 | 2. 1 | 40. 15 || Is. 14. 12 || Ez. 28. 16 | 31. 8 Hab. 1. 4 *l* || S. Luke 10. 18 || 1 S. Pet. 5. 8.

204. *That tribulation is to be embraced for the sake of* GOD.

Job 5. 17 || Ps. 23. 4 *l* || S. Matt. 5. 10 || S. James 1. 2.

(76)

205. *That God chastens those whom He loves.*

Deut. 32. 39 ‖ Job 1. 8, 12 | 7. 18 ‖ Ps. 60. 3
66. 11 | 89. 31, 32 ‖ Prov. 3. 11 ‖ Is. 49. 2
Jer. 30. 11 ‖ 46. 28 ‖ Hos. 6. 1 ‖ Mic. 4. 13
Wis. 2. 20 | Ecclus. 30. 1 ‖ Bar. 4. 26 ‖ 2 Macc.
6. 13 ‖ S. Matt. 10. 16 ‖ S. Luke 10. 3 ‖ S. John
2. 15 | 2 Cor. 7. 5 | 11. 23 *l* ‖ Eph. 2. 14 ‖ Heb.
12. 5, 7 ‖ Rev. 3. 19.

206. *That the Lord sometimes spares out of anger.*

Job 21. 7, 9 ‖ Is. 5. 6 *f* | 14. 29 *f* | 26. 10 *f*
Ez. 16. 42 ‖ Hos. 4. 14 ‖ Heb. 12. 8.

207. *That the Saints consider temporal affliction to be a blessing and rejoice in it.*

Ex. 15. 24 ‖ Lev. 11. 9 ‖ Deut. 33. 18 ‖ Judg. 7. 20
Job. 6. 8, 9 | 39. 21 ‖ Ps. 18. 35 *l* | 23. 4 | 77. 3
Cant. 1. 5, 13 ‖ Jer. 15. 18 ‖ Lam. 3. 30 ‖ Ecclus.
29. 10 ‖ 2 Macc. 6. 20 ‖ Acts 5. 41 | 20. 22, 23
21. 13 ‖ Rom. 5. 3 ‖ 2 Cor. 4. 8 | 6. 10 | 8. 2 | 12. 9
Heb. 10. 34 ‖ S. James 1. 2.

208. *That God is often sought in tribulation.*

Gen. 7. 17 | 19. 16 ‖ Ex. 12. 33 ‖ Deut. 30. 1
Judg. 10. 10 | 11. 4, 6 ‖ 1 Sam. 22. 2 | 30. 10
2 Chron. 33. 12 ‖ Job 42. 5 ‖ Ps. 60. 3 ‖ Is. 26. 9 *l*, 16
43. 6 ‖ Jer. 46. 15 ‖ Lam. 1. 8 *l* ‖ Hos. 2. 7, 14
Zech. 3. 3 ‖ S. Luke 14. 23 | 15. 16, 17.

210. *That tribulation instructs.*

2 Chron. 33. 13 *l* ‖ Prov. 22. 15, 29 *f* ‖ Is. 8. 11 *f*
Ecclus. 31. 2 ‖ Bar. 2. 18, 30 *l*.

210 *That tribulation increases and fertilizes.*

Gen. 9. 1 ‖ Ex. 1. 12 *f* ‖ 2 Kings 2. 20 ‖ Job 9. 8 *l*
Is. 54. 16 ‖ Dan. 3. 24, 25 ‖ S. John 15. 2
2 Cor. 4. 16.

(77)

211. *That tribulation examines and purges.*

Deut. 8. 16 *l* ‖ Job 6. 4 | 23. 10 | 33. 19 | Ps. 17. 3 *f* | Is. 1. 25 | 4. 4 | 40. 2 ‖ Mal. 3. 2 *l* ‖ Wis. 2. 19 | Ecclus. 27. 5 ‖ S. Matt. 3. 12 ‖ 1 S. Pet. 1. 7.

212. *That tribulation defends.*

Ex. 14. 22 *l* ‖ 1 Sam. 27. 4 ‖ 1 Kings 17. 3 | Job 2. 13 | Ps. 60. 11 ‖ Cant. 2. 14.

213. *That tribulation crowns.*

Gen. 35. 10 ‖ Job 12. 5 ‖ Prov. 20. 14 | 31. 25 | Is. 14. 3 | 54. 7 ‖ Jer. 30. 17 ‖ Hos. 14. 7 ‖ S. Matt. 5. 10 | 16. 2 ‖ S. Luke 24. 26 ‖ S. John 7. 8 | Rom. 8. 18 ‖ 2 Cor. 4. 10, 17 ‖ 2 Tim. 2. 5 | Heb. 12. 11 ‖ S. James 1. 12 ‖ 1 S. Pet. 4. 17.

214. *That by tribulation a man is known.*

Ex. 1. 12 *f* ‖ Judg. 3. 1 ‖ Ps. 17. 3 | 94. 12 | Prov. 20. 30 | 25. 4 ‖ Eccles. 1. 18 ‖ Zech. 13. 9 | Wis. 3. 5 ‖ Ecclus. 2. 5 | 27. 5.

215. *If the righteous are afflicted in this present life, how great shall be the punishment of the wicked in the life to come.*

Prov. 11. 21 ‖ Is. 9. 17 *f* | 32. 13 ‖ Jer. 12. 1 *l* | 25. 29 *f* | 49. 12 ‖ Ez. 9. 6 ‖ Joel 3. 16 ‖ Mal. 3. 2 *l* | S. Luke 23. 31 ‖ 1 S. Pet. 4. 17.

216. *Of the comparison of prosperity with adversity.*

Gen. 40. 14, 23 | Ex. 13. 21 ‖ Job 3. 20 | Ps. 42. 10 | 66. 11 | Prov. 30. 8 ‖ Is. 43. 6 ‖ Jer. 48. 11 | Ecclus. 32. 10 ‖ S. James 4. 4 *l*.

217. *That in evil prosperity we must not be puffed up, and in good adversity we must not despair.*

Gen. 12. 8 *m* ‖ Deut. 24. 6 | Job 11. 17 ‖ Ecclus. 11. 27 | 18. 25 | 38. 9 | S. Luke 21. 28.

218. *Against those who call upon* GOD *in adversity and not in prosperity.*

Ex. 8. 8 | 10. 7 ‖ Lev. 8. 35 ‖ 1 Sam. 6. 12 *m* Ps. 119. 43 ' Is. 20. 12 | 29. 9, 16 | 38. 18 | 57. 10 62. 6 ‖ Jer. 31. 21 ‖ Hos. 5. 15 ‖ Hab. 2. 1.

219. *That prosperity is the cause of pride, luxury, and forgetfulness of the mercies of* GOD.

Gen. 13. 6 ‖ Num. 11. 33 ‖ Deut. 6. 10, 12 8. 10. 11 | 20. 13 | 32. 15 *f* ‖ Judg. 11. 2 ‖ 1 Sam. 15. 12 Job. 12. 6 ‖ Ps. 73. 12 ‖ Prov. 1. 32 *l* 30. 9 *f* ‖ Is. 2. 7, 8 | Jer. 2. 7 | 46. 6 | 48. 11 Ezek. 16. 14, 15 ‖ Hos. 10. 1 *m* ‖ Mic. 6. 11 ‖ Hab. 1. 10 ‖ Ecclus. 47. 20.

220. *That many are the afflictions of the righteous, but the* LORD *delivereth him out of all.*

Gen. 31. 29 | 32. 11 ‖ Ex. 10. 10 ‖ 1 Sam. 23. 26, 27 ‖ 1 Kings 19. 4 ‖ 2 Kings 7. 6 ‖ Ps. 3. 1, 6 17. 3 | 18. 3 | 31. 8 *l* | 50. 15 | 55. 5 | 57. 4 | 60. 3 66. 9, 11 | 71. 18 | 86. 14 | 88. 15 | 89. 31, 32 94. 19 | 102. 4, 17 | 120. 1 ‖ Jer. 38. 13 ‖ Sus. 62 *l* Bel. 38 ‖ 2 Macc. 10. 29 ‖ S. John 16. 33 ‖ Acts 5. 19 | 12. 6 | 27. 22.

221. *That* GOD *comforts the afflicted and distressed, and in his wrath remembers mercy.*

Gen. 5. 29 ‖ 2 Chron. 34. 27 | Ps. 34. 18 | 91. 15 *l* Prov. 12. 25 ‖ Is. 61. 1 *l* | 66. 13 ‖ Mic. 5. 5 *f* S. John 16. 1 ‖ 2 Cor. 1. 3.

222. *That the* LORD *fights for them that are His.*

Ex. 14. 14, 25 | 15. 3 | 23. 22 ‖ Deut. 1. 30 | 3. 30 4. 3 *l* | 20. 2 | 31. 3 ‖ Josh. 6. 20 | 10. 11 *l* | 23. 10 *l* Judg. 4. 15 | 5. 20 ‖ 1 Sam 7. 10 ‖ 2 Kings 19. 35 2 Chron. 32. 8 Neh. 4. 15 ‖ Ps. 3. 7 | 24. 8 35. 2 | 44. 8 | Prov. 3. 26 ‖ Is. 37. 36 ‖ Jer. 20. 11 *f* Jud. 5. 21 ‖ 2 Macc. 8. 25 | 10. 29 | 11. 8 | 12. 22 15. 16 ‖ Rev. 2. 16.

223. *That all victory, temporal or spiritual, is to be ascribed to* GOD.

> Ex. 15. 3 ‖ Judg. 15. 18 ‖ 1 Sam. 17. 17 *l*
> 2 Chron. 14. 11 | 28. 8 *l* ‖ Ps. 3. 8 *f* | 18. 40
> Prov. 21. 31 ‖ Jud. 9. 11 | 16. 6 ‖ 1 Macc. 3. 18
> Rom. 16. 20 *f*.

224. *Of good habits and perseverance in good.*

> Gen. 37. 3 ‖ Ex. 24. 12 | 27. 1 ‖ Lev. 6. 21
> Num. 11. 1 *l* ‖ Josh. 5. 8 | Judg. 5. 20 *l* Ruth 2. 7 *l*
> Job 1. 5 | 27. 6 Ps. 1. 3 | 108. 2 ‖ Is. 21. 8 | 54. 2
> Jer. 3. 19 *l* ‖ Hab. 2. 1 ‖ Ecclus. 2. 1, 13 | 4. 28
> 51. 30 ‖ S. Mark 9. 5 S. Luke 22. 28 ‖ Rom. 8. 38
> 1 Cor. 9. 24 *l* | 16. 13 ‖ Gal. 6. 9 ‖ Eph. 3. 13
> 2 Thess. 3. 13 ‖ Heb. 10. 35.

225. *Of maturity or constancy.*

> Job. 28. 25 | 29. 8, 24 ‖ Ps. 35. 18 | 119. 147
> Tob. 3. 15 Ecclus. 19. 30 | 27. 11 ‖ 1 Cor. 13. 11
> 1 Tim. 4. 12 *f* | 2 Tim. 2. 22 ‖ Tit. 2. 7.

226. *Of the hope of the everlasting reward; or that the Saints are fed by the expectation of things eternal.*

> Ex. 9. 32 ‖ Job 14. 14 | 19. 25 ‖ Prov. 10. 28 *f*
> 13. 21 *l* | 20. 21 ‖ Is. 30. 18 *l* | 33. 2 64. 4
> Jer. 31. 30 ‖ Hos. 3. 3 | 11. 7 | Hab. 2. 3 ‖ Ecclus. 2. 9
> 11. 25 | 20. 16 *m* ‖ S. Luke 16. 25 ‖ Tit. 2. 13
> Heb. 11. 26 *l* | S. James 5. 7 2 S. Pet. 3. 9.

227. *Of the reward of the good; or the everlasting vestment of the body and the soul.*

> Gen. 6. 14 ‖ Ps. 87. 2 | 89. 35 ‖ Haggai 2. 9
> Rev. 12. 1 | 21. 23.

228. *Of our being arrayed with good works, and of the ornament of grace and glory according to the* HOLY GHOST; *or that our garments must be white at all times.*

Gen. 24. 22 | 27. 14 | 41. 14 | 45. 22 ‖ Ex. 19. 10 Ruth 3. 3 ‖ 1 Sam. 2. 18 2 Sam. 1. 24 ‖ Esth. 5. 1 6. 8 ‖ Job 29. 14 ‖ Prov. 31. 21 ‖ Eccles. 9. 8 Cant. 1. 11 ‖ Is. 52. 1 | 61. 10 ‖ Jer. 2. 32 | 31. 4 Ezek. 16 10. ‖ Zech. 3. 4 ‖ Jud. 10. 3 ‖ Wis. 18. 24 1 Macc. 10. 20 ‖ S. Matt. 17. 2 ‖ S. John 19. 40 Rev. 1. 13 | 3. 4, 18 | 7. 9 *l*, 13 | 10. 1 | 19. 8, 11.

229. *Of everlasting beatitude; or, of the ineffableness of eternal joy.*

Ps. 31. 21 | 42. 4 | 73. 24 | 84. 1 | 102. 3 | 122. 1 126. 6 | Is. 8. 18 | 24. 16 *f* | 30. 26 | 33. 17 | 35. 10 51. 3 | 60. 19 | 61. 7 | 64. 4 ‖ Dan. 12. 3 ‖ Wis. 3. 7 15. 3 ‖ Bar. 3. 24 ‖ S. Matt. 22. 29 | 25. 34 S. Luke 6. 38 | 9. 33 | 12. 37 | S. John 16. 22 | 17. 3 Acts 7. 55 ‖ 1 Cor. 2. 9. ‖ Col. 2. 9 ‖ Rev. 2. 7, 17 5. 8 | 7. 16 | 14. 2 | 21. 4, 18, 23.

SECOND PART.

230. *Against instability of heart; or, against inconstancy and wandering of thought.*

Gen. 4. 14 | 8. 7 | 25. 27 | 34. 1 ‖ Ex. 9. 19 12. 22 *l* ‖ Josh. 2. 19 2 Kings 6. 9 ‖ Job 29. 19 31. 5 ‖ Ps. 1. 5 ‖ Prov. 27. 8 Is. 22. 18 | 41. 7 *l* 57. 20 ‖ Jer. 14. 10 | 52. 3 ‖ Lam. 1. 8 ‖ Mic. 1. 13 Ecclus. 5. 9, 10 | 6. 24 | 14. 25 | 27. 11 | 33. 5 36. 26 S. Luke 15. 13 ‖ 2 Thess. 2. 2 | 3. 11 Heb. 13. 9 *f* ‖ S. James 1. 6 *l* ‖ 1 S. John 4. 1.

231. *Against idolators; or that none can serve* GOD *and Mammon.*

Gen. 35. 2 || Ex. 20. 3 || Lev. 26. 1 || Deut. 12. 3 | 1 Sam. 5. 3 || 1 Kings 11. 4 || Ps. 81. 9, 10 | Is. 28. 20 | 49. 20 *l* || Hos. 9. 10 || Amos 3. 3 | Zeph. 1. 5 || Zech. 11. 8 || Ecclus. 2. 12 | 13. 18 | S. Matt. 6. 24 | 8. 29 || 1 Cor. 10. 14 || 2 Cor. 6. 15 | Philip. 3. 19 || S. James 1. 8.

232. *Against those that mix good with evil.*

Ez. 14. 28 || Lev. 1. 2 | 22. 4 || Deut. 18. 13 | 1 Sam. 15. 3 || Neh. 13. 15 || Job. 31. 7 || Ps. 1. 4 | 106. 11 | 119. 101 ' Eccles. 9. 10 || Cant. 4. 7 | Is. 1. 22 | 5. 20 || Ecclus. 33. 22 || 1 Macc. 4. 42 | 7. 46 *l* | 9. 10 || 2 Macc. 6. 24 || S. Matt. 23. 25 | 1 Cor. 10. 21 || S. James 2. 10.

233. *Against those who too often frequent the houses of their friends, and of great men.*

2 Sam. 19. 34 || Prov. 25. 17 || Ecclus. 13. 9 | 21. 22.

234. *Against the natural desire of often visiting our relations, and dwelling too much with them.*

Gen. 12. 1 | 13. 14 | 19. 14, 16 | 47. 24 || Ex. 32. 27 | Lev. 21. 1 || Deut. 33. 9 | 1 Sam. 6. 10, 12 | 2 Sam. 11. 11 || Ps. 45. 11 || Prov. 25. 16 || Jer. 9. 4 | Joel 1. 4 || Mic. 7. 5 || 2 Macc. 15. 18 || S. Matt. 8. 21 | 12. 47, 48 | 18. 8 , S. Mark 3. 32 || S. Luke 2. 49 | 8. 21 | 9. 61 ; S. John 2. 4 || Heb. 7. 3.

235. *That if we return to sin, the devil assaults us more vehemently; or, against backsliding.*

Gen. 19. 26 ; Ex. 16. 2, 3 || Num. 11. 5 || Job 31. 1 | Prov. 26. 11 || Jer. 15. 6 Lam. 1. 13 || Ezek. 1. 12 | Dan. 11. 13 || Hos. 8. 3, 13 || Amos 4. 11 || S. Matt. 12. 43 | 24. 17 || S. Luke 9. 62 | 11. 24 | 17. 31, 32 | S. John 5. 14 | 8. 11 || Gal. 3. 3 || Heb. 6. 4 | 10. 29 | 2 S. Pet. 2. 22.

236. *That one who has fallen back into sin may often profit the righteous.*

Job 8. 7 ‖ Ps. 119. 67, 71 ‖ Ecclus. 4. 25 | 42. 14 Rom. 5. 21 | 8. 28.

237. *Concerning evil habit and obstinacy; or, that an inveterate custom is with great difficulty given up.*

Ex. 16. 3 ‖ Num. 11. 5 | 14. 3 *l* ‖ Job 18. 8 Prov. 27. 22 ‖ Is. 5. 18 | 58. 6 ‖ Jer. 2. 32 *l* | 3. 3 6. 15 | 8. 4 | 9. 5 *l* | 13. 23 | 17. 1 ‖ Lam. 3. 27, 53 4. 8 ‖ Ez. 24. 12 ‖ Zech. 5. 7 ‖ Ecclus. 26. 28 *l* S. Mark 9. 26 ‖ S. Luke 9. 39 ‖ S. John 11. 43 Rom. 2. 4 | 6. 21.

231. *Against obstinate old men.*

1 Sam. 3. 18 ‖ Job 6. 15 ‖ Is. 65. 20 ‖ Ezek. 8. 12 Hos. 7. 9.

239. *Of the bodies of the wicked; that they are altogether polluted with sin.*

Gen. 6. 16 | Ex. 9. 9 ‖ Num. 12. 10 ‖ Deut. 27. 18 28. 22 ‖ Job. 2. 7 | 41. 14 ‖ Ps. 109. 17 ‖ Is. 1. 5, 6 53. 2 *l* ‖ 2 Macc. 9. 5 ‖ S. Matt. 8. 2 ‖ S. Luke 5. 12 8. 27.

240. *Concerning the bitterness of the life of the wicked.*

Ex. 5. 6 | 8. 24 ‖ Deut. 28. 65 ‖ Judg. 16. 21 Job 30. 7 ‖ Is. 42. 25 | 57. 20 | 59. 8 *f* ‖ Jer. 2. 19 *m* 5. 3 | 9. 5 *l* | 16. 13 *l* ‖ Lam. 1. 20 | 3. 5 | 5. 5 Hos. 7. 9 *f* | 10. 11 *l* ‖ Wis. 5. 7 ‖ S. Mark 5. 5 S. Luke 15. 16 ‖ Rev. 8. 11 | 14. 11.

241. *That the wicked neither feel nor care for the labour which they undergo for the world.*

Prov. 23. 34 ‖ Hos. 7. 9.

242. *Of watchfulness.*

Deut. 4. 9 ‖ 2 Sam. 21. 10 ‖ Ps. 59. 9 | 119. 109 127. 1 | 130. 6 ‖ Prov. 4. 23 | 27. 18 *f* ‖ Is. 21. 8 Jer. 17. 21 *f* ‖ Hab. 2. 1 ‖ Bar. 3. 34 ‖ S. Luke 11. 21 ‖ 1 Thess. 4. 4 ‖ Heb. 3. 13.

243. *That those who are unfruitful will be cut off; or that we ought to avoid the companionship, counsels, conversation, and example of the wicked.*

Gen. 3. 4, 6, 12 | 11. 3 *f* | 12. 1 | 14. 11 | 21. 9 26. 23 | 27. 43 | 49. 5 ‖ Lev. 18. 3 ‖ Num. 16. 26 25. 1 ‖ 1 Sam. 15. 6 ‖ 1 Kings 12. 8 ‖ 2 Chron. 19. 2 20. 37 *m* | 24. 17 ‖ Job. 6. 27 | 16. 2 | 21. 16 *l* Ps. 1. 1 | 6. 8 | 101. 8, 10 ‖ Prov. 1. 10 | 2. 11, 12 4. 14 | 13. 20 | 23. 6 | 24. 1, 21 *l* ‖ Jer. 48. 28 49. 8 | 51. 6 ‖ Obad. 7 ‖ Ecclus. 8. 5, 18 | 10. 2 11. 32 | 13. 1, 17 | 22. 13 | 25. 16 | 37. 8 | 41. 8 1 Macc. 2. 27 ‖ S. Matt. 2. 9 | 18. 8 ‖ S. Mark 8. 15 9. 18 ‖ S. Luke 10. 11 ‖ Rom. 12. 2 ‖ 1 Cor. 5. 2 *l* 15. 33 ‖ 2 Thess. 3. 6 | 3. 10.

244. *That the sin of one man is often visited on many.*

Gen. 3. 17 and Rom. 5. 12 ‖ Num. 32. 15 ‖ Josh. 7. 24 ‖ Judg. 20 and 21; for the sin of Gibeon, the whole tribe of Benjamin is destroyed. 1 Sam. 4, for the sin of the sons of Eli, 30,000 Israelites are slain, and the ark is taken. 2 Sam. 21. 1 | 24; for the sin of David in numbering the people, 70,000 are slain.

245. *That we are sometimes to tolerate the company of the wicked.*

Gen. 13. 12 *l* ‖ Job. 1. 1 | 30. 29 ‖ Ps. 31. 13 41. 9 ‖ Cant. 2. 2 ‖ Is. 6. 5 *m* ‖ Ez. 2. 6 ‖ S. Mark 9. 19 ‖ S. Luke 22. 21 ‖ 2 S. Pet. 2. 7 ‖ Rev. 2. 13 *f*

246. *That we are to seek for the companionship of the good, and for religious confraternities.*

Gen. 21. 32 ‖ Ruth 1. 16 | 2 Chron. 15. 9 | Job. 5. 23 ‖ Prov. 13. 20 *f* ‖ Eccles. 4. 9 ‖ Ecclus. 6. 35 | 9. 15 *f* | 24. 16 | 37. 12 ‖ S. Matt. 12. 42 | S. John 1, 38, 39 ‖ Acts 9. 26 ‖ S. James 5. 16.

247. *Of the usefulness of good companionship.*

Gen. 18. 32 | 30. 30 | 39. 5 ‖ Ex. 34. 30 ‖ Judg. 17. 13 ¦ 2 Sam. 6. 11 ‖ Job. 42. 8 ‖ Is. 37. 35.

248. *That no evil shall go unpunished, and no good shall remain unrewarded.*

Job 4. 8 | 36. 11. 12 ‖ Prov. 11. 18, 27 *l* | Eccles. 12. 14 ‖ Wis. 3. 15 ‖ Ecclus. 51. 30 ‖ Rom. 1. 18 | 6. 22 ‖ 2 Cor. 9. 6 ‖ Gal. 5. 21 *l* | 6. 5, 9 | 2 S. Pet. 2. 2 ‖ Rev. 22. 12.

249. *That the greatest men will suffer the greatest punishment.*

Lev. 21. 9 ‖ Is. 2. 12 | 34. 6 ‖ Amos. 9. 1 ‖ Wis. 6. 6 *l* ‖ Ecclus. 12. 13 ‖ S. Matt. 23. 14 *l* ‖ Rev. 18. 7, 8 | 19. 17, 18.

250. *That punishment will answer to crime both in quantity and quality.*

Judg. 1. 7 ‖ Ps. 5. 11 | 7. 17 | 62. 12 *l* ¦ Is. 33. 1 | Jer. 21. 14 *f* | 25. 14 *l* | 30. 14 | 32. 19 ‖ Ez. 31. 10, 11 ‖ Joel 3. 4 *l* ‖ Wis. 11. 16 ‖ 1 Macc. 2. 67 | 2 Macc. 5. 10 | 9. 28 ‖ S. Mark 4. 24 *m* ‖ S. Luke 6. 38 *l* ‖ Rev. 18. 6.

251. *That after they are cast into hell, the eyes of the wicked will be opened.*

Job 21. 20 | 27. 19 ‖ Ps. 9. 17 | 78. 34 ‖ Is. 2. 20 | Wis. 5. 2 *f*, 8 ¦ S. Luke 16. 23.

BOOK IV.

First Part.

252. *Of prudence, which is called discretion.*

Gen. 4. 7 | 24. 65 *l* ‖ Josh. 1. 7 | 11. 6 *l* 1 Chron. 19. 10 ‖ Prov. 2. 3 | 3. 13 | 4. 1, 7, 25 8. 1 | 11. 12 | 14. 6, 15 | 16. 16 | 17. 10, 24 | 20. 5 24. 3 | 27. 12, 19 | 28. 16 | Eccles. 9. 18 ‖ Ecclus. 38. 4 ‖ S. Matt. 10. 16 ‖ 1 Tim. 5. 23 ‖ 1 S. Pet. 4. 7.

253. *Of temperance.*

1 Chron. 13. 9 ‖ Dan. 1. 12 | 10. 2 ‖ Tob. 4. 13 Jud. 8. 6 ‖ Ecclus. 31. 19 | 37. 29 ‖ 1 Tim. 3. 11 Tit. 2. 6, 12.

254. *Of fortitude.*

Gen. 32. 28 | 49. 14 ‖ Josh. 1. 6 | 10. 25 ‖ Judg. 6. 12 ‖ 1 Sam. 30. 6 ‖ 2 Sam. 22. 23 ‖ 1 Kings 19. 8 | 1 Chron. 11. 11 *f* ‖ 2 Chron. 16. 9 *f* ‖ Neh. 8. 10 *l* ‖ Job. 6. 11 | 38. 3 | 39. 19 ‖ Ps. 27. 16 31. 27 | 105. 36 ‖ 108. 1 ‖ Prov. 10. 4 | 20. 9 *f* 24. 5 | 28. 1 *l* | 30. 30 | 31. 17, 25 ‖ Cant. 3. 7 Is. 7. 21 | 12. 2 | 35. 3 | 40. 31 | 41. 6 | 51. 7 52. 1 ‖ Joel 3. 10 ‖ Jud. 15. 10 | 16. 10 | Ecclus. 7. 10 | 46. 1 | 47. 3 ‖ 2 Macc. 6. 31 | S. Matt. 11. 12 2 Cor. 4. 8 ‖ Philip. 4. 13 ‖ 2 Tim. 2. 1.

255. *Of justice.*

Deut. 25. 13 | 27. 19 | Job. 17. 9 | 31. 21 ‖ Ps. 45. 8 | 72. 1 | 82. 3 | 85. 13 | 92. 11 | 101. 4 Prov. 2. 21 | 3. 3 | 11. 5, 8 | 13. 25 | 20. 10 | 31. 9 Is. 16. 5 *l* | 42. 3 *l* | 59, 14, 17 ‖ Jer. 22. 3

Ezek. 33. 19 ‖ Hos. 10. 12 *f* ‖ Mic. 6. 8. 11 ‖ Zech. 7. 9 | 8. 16 ‖ Ecclus. 4. 9, 28 | 7. 3 | 35. 3, 12.

256. *Of the balance of justice.*
Of thought, which weighs cogitations.

Ps. 97. 11ᶜ | 103. 17 ‖ Prov. 10. 6 | 11. 9.

Of speech, which ponders that which is said, or is to be said.

Ps. 58. 1 | 141. 5 | 145. 17 ‖ Prov. 10. 11 | 31. 8.

Of operation, which weighs that which is done, or to be done.

Gen. 2. 10 ‖ Ex. 28. 17 ‖ Lev. 19. 35 ‖ Ps. 11. 8 58. 9 | 82. 3 | 112. 9 ‖ Prov. 11. 1 | 12. 21 | 20. 23 28. 1 ‖ Is. 1. 21 ‖ Ezek. 45. 10 ‖ Wis. 1. 1 | 5. 1 10. 6, 10 ‖ Sus. 48. 53.

Second Part.

257. *Of faith and its articles; otherwise of the Sacraments.*

Gen. 15. 6 ‖ Is. 11. 5 *l* | 28. 16 *l* | 53. 1 ‖ Jer. 17. 5, 7 ‖ Hab. 2. 4 *l* ‖ S. Matt. 7. 25 *l* | 8. 13 9. 29 | 13. 33 | 15. 28 | 16. 18 | 17. 19, 20 | 21. 32 S. Mark 5. 34 | 9. 23 | 11. 22 | 16. 16 ‖ S. Luke 17. 6 | 18. 8 *l*, 42 ‖ S. John 1. 12, 50 | 3. 15 *l*, 18 4. 53 *l* | 5. 24 | 6. 40 | 7. 38 | 8. 24 | 9. 35 11. 25 *l* | 12. 42 | 14. 12 | 16. 30 *l* | 17. 20 | 20. 31 Acts 15. 9 ‖ Rom. 1. 17 *l* | 3. 22 | 4. 3, 23 | 5. 1 9. 30 | 10. 10, 11 | 11. 20 *l* ‖ 1 Cor. 3. 11 ‖ Gal. 3. 11 ‖ Eph. 6. 16 ‖ Col. 1. 23 *f* ‖ 1 Thess. 1. 3 *f* 3. 5 | 5. 8 ‖ 2 Thess. 1. 4 ‖ 1. Tim. 1. 19 | 4. 12 *l* 2 Tim. 1. 5 *f*. 13 | 3. 10 ‖ Tit. 1. 16 | 2. 1 ‖ Heb. 4. 2 *l* | 10. 38 | 11. 1 ‖ S. James 2. 17, 19 ‖ 1 S. Pet. 1. 5, 8 ‖ 1 S. John 5. 1 ‖ S. Jude 3. 20.

258. *Of hope.*
Job 5. 16 | 13. 15 | 14. 7, 14 | 19. 25 ‖ Ps. 5. 12
9. 10 | 21. 7 | 22. 9 | 23. 4 | 27. 3 | 30. 1
31. 1 | 33. 18 | 37. 3, 5 | 38. 15 | 39. 8 | 40. 5 | 43. 7
52. 9 | 55. 23 | 56. 4 | 57. 1 | 73. 27 | 78. 8
84. 13 | 91. 2, 14 | 119. 43 *l* | 130. 5 ‖ Prov. 10. 28
14. 32 *l* ‖ Is. 40. 31 | 64. 4 ‖ Jer. 17. 7, 17 ‖ Hos.
2. 15 ‖ Ecclus. 2. 9, 14 ‖ Rom. 5. 5 *f* | 12. 12 *f*
1 Tim. 1. 1 *l* ‖ Heb. 4. 16 ‖ S. James 1. 6 | 5. 7
S. Pet. 1. 3, 21 *l* | 3. 5.

259. *Of charity.*
Lev. 6. 13 | 19. 18, 34 ‖ Deut. 6. 5 | 10. 12
11. 13 | 30. 6 ‖ Prov. 3. 28 | 8. 17 | 10. 12 | 17. 17
18. 24 ‖ Cant. 1. 4 *l*, 7 *f* | 2. 3, 8, 16 | 31. 10
5. 8 | 7. 10 | 8. 6 ‖ Jer. 31. 3 ‖ Dan. 9. 4 ‖ Ecclus.
6. 14 | 7. 35 | 9. 10 | 13. 14 | 22. 21 | 24. 18 | 25. 1
27. 17 | 34. 16 | 37. 6 | 44. 10 | 47. 8 *l* ‖ S.
Matt. 5. 44 | 22. 37 ‖ S. Luke 6. 27 | 7. 47 | 10. 27
S. John 13. 34, 35 | 14. 15, 21, 23 | 15. 10, 12
21. 16 ‖ Rom. 5. 5 *l* | 8. 35 | 12. 9 *f* | 13. 8 ‖ 1 Cor.
8. 1 *l* | 13. 1 ‖ 2 Cor. 12. 15 ‖ Gal. 5. 14, 22 ‖ Eph.
3. 19 ‖ Philip. 2. 1 ‖ Col. 1. 4 | 2. 2 | 3. 14 ‖ 1 Thess.
1. 3 | 3. 6 | 4. 9 ‖ 2 Thess. 1. 3 | 3. 5 ‖ 1 Tim. 1. 5
4. 12 ‖ Heb. 13. 1 ‖ S. James 2. 8 ‖ 1 S. Pet.
1. 22 | 2. 17 | 4. 8 ‖ 1 S. John 2. 10, 15 *l* | 3. 11, 17,
18 | 4. 8, 11 ‖ 2 S. John 6 ‖ S. Jude 21 *f*.

260. *Of the love of* God *and one's neighbour.*
Prov. 10. 12 *l* ‖ Cant. 8. 2 ‖ S. Luke 12. 49
Rom. 13. 10 ‖ 1 Cor. 13. 4 | 14. 1 ‖ 1 Tim. 1. 5
Rev. 3. 18.

261. *Against despair.*
Gen. 4. 13 ‖ 2 Sam. 2. 26 ‖ 2 Kings 20. 1 ‖ Ps.
77. 2 *l* ‖ Prov. 4. 27 | 24. 10 ‖ Is. 38. 1 | 51. 17
Jer. 2. 25 | 3. 12 | 18. 8 | 38. 10 ‖ Ezek. 18. 27,
32 ‖ Hos. 2. 19 ‖ Jon. 1. 17 ‖ Zech. 8. 6 ‖ Ecclus.
2. 10 | 11. 25 *l* | 38. 9 ‖ S. Luke 7. 37 | 22. 62
23. 42 ‖ Acts 9. 1 ‖ S. Jude 11 *f*.

262. *Of the pusillanimity of the wicked.*

Ex. 15. 16 ƒ ‖ Lev. 26. 36 ‖ Deut. 28. 66 ‖ Josh. 2. 11 | 5. 1 ‖ 1 Sam. 4. 7 | 25. 37 ‖ Job. 15. 24 18. 11 ‖ Ps. 53. 6 ‖ Prov. 28. 1 ‖ Jer. 20. 3 *l* ‖ Hos. 7. 11 ‖ Wis. 17. 4 ‖ S. John 10. 12.

263. *Against an evil fear.*

Prov. 10. 24 ‖ Is. 41. 14 ‖ Ecclus. 22. 18 S. Matt. 10. 28 ‖ S. Luke 12. 32.

264. *Of presumption.*

Ex. 3. 3 | 19. 12 ‖ Lev. 10. 1 | 22. 3 ‖ 2 Sam. 6. 6 ‖ 2 Chron. 26. 18 ‖ Prov. 18. 13 | 25. 6 Ecclus. 7. 5 | 8. 14 | 11. 7 | 31. 12 ‖ S. Matt. 7. 3 8. 8 | 22. 12.

265. *Of the security of the righteous.*

Job 1. 10 | 5. 22 | 11. 15 | 39. 21 ‖ Ps. 3. 7 23. 4 | 27. 1, 3 | 34. 7, 22 | 46. 2 | 91. 4 | 140. 7 Prov. 3. 25 | 28. 1 *l* | 30. 30 ‖ Ecclus. 34. 16 1 S. John 4. 4.

266. *That the righteous ought not to fear the powerful, but rather despise them for* GOD'S *sake; or, of a good fear.*

Deut. 5. 29 | 10. 12 ‖ 1 Sam. 4. 7 | 18. 12 2 Kings 17. 38 ‖ Job 1. 1 *l* | 7. 13, 14 | 9. 28 | 13. 11 25. 2 | 26. 11 | 28. 28 | 37. 1 ‖ Ps. 2. 11 | 19. 9 22. 23 | 25. 11 | 34. 7, 11 | 102. 15 | 111. 5 | 112. 1 128. 1 ‖ Prov. 1. 7 | 10. 27 | 14. 16 | 16. 6 *l* 28. 14 ƒ ‖ Eccles. 12. 13 ‖ Is. 66. 2 *l* ‖ Jer. 5. 24 Mal. 1. 6 ‖ Tob. 4. 21 ‖ Ecclus. 1. 13, 20 | 2. 7, 8, 9, 17 | 3. 7 | 10. 22 | 15. 1 | 16. 2 | 18. 27 | 23. 27 27. 4 | 33. 1 | 34. 14 | 40. 27 ‖ S. Mark 6. 20 Acts 10. 35 ‖ 1 S. Pet. 1. 17 *l* | 2. 17 ‖ Rev. 14. 7.

267. *That* GOD *sees not only deeds, but also thoughts, and is therefore to be feared.*

Num. 14. 28 | Is. 50. 8 | 57. 11 | 65. 3 ‖ Jer. 8. 6 23. 23 ‖ Ecclus. 17. 15 | 23. 19 ‖ S. James 5. 9 *l.*

(89)

Third Part.

268. *Of the active life as regards good works; or, of the labour of the hands.*

Gen. 3. 19 ‖ Job 17. 9 ‖ Ps. 128. 2 ׀ Prov. 6. 6 31. 17, 27 ‖ Ecclus. 7. 15 ‖ 1 Thess. 4. 11 *l* ‖ Eph. 4. 28 ׀ 2 Thess. 3. 8, 10.

269. *Of the caution and judgment to be employed in doing good works.*

Lev. 2. 13 ‖ Josh. 5. 13 *l* | 11. 9 | 1 Sam. 4. 3 Job 13. 14 ‖ Prov. 23. 1 | 28. 5 | 31. 13 ‖ Cant. 5. 5 Is. 30. 21 ‖ Ecclus. 17. 5 ׀ S. Mark 9. 50 S. Luke 14. 34 ‖ Rom. 12. 1 *l* ‖ 1 Cor. 11. 31 ‖ 1 Tim. 5. 23 S. James 3. 17 ‖ 1 S. John 4. 1.

270. *That we must labour before we can rest.*

Gen. 26. 12 | 32. 28 | 35. 28 ‖ Lev. 23. 14 2 Sam. 7. 1 ‖ 2 Kings 2. 11 ׀ Ps. 66. 11 | 110. 7 124. 6 ׀ Ecclus. 24. 15 ‖ S. Mark 10. 38 ׀ S. Luke 24. 26.

271. *That the understanding of good works is rightly given to those who are pure and humble.*

Gen. 18. 1 | 35. 7 *l* | 47. 16 ‖ Ex. 19. 21 Deut. 33. 3 ׀ Judg. 6. 11 ‖ Job 22. 23 ‖ Ps. 45. 11 65. 14 ‖ Prov. 2. 3 | 3. 32 | 16. 22 ‖ Eccles. 2. 3 5. 1 ‖ Is. 6. 1 | 8. 16 | 11. 8 | 50. 4 | 55. 3 Dan. 1. 16, 17 ‖ Ecclus. 1. 26 | 5. 11 ‖ S. Matt. 3. 16 11. 25 ‖ S. Luke 10. 2, 39 ‖ 2 Cor. 3. 15 ‖ Rev. 1. 12.

272. *That a blessing is given to those who do good deeds.*

Gen. 27. 27 | 28. 4 ‖ 2 Kings 20. 2 Job 29. 13 31. 20 ‖ Judith 10. 7 ‖ S. Matt. 26. 26 ‖ S. Luke 22. 19.

273. *Of good savour and good fame.*

Gen. 8. 21 | 27. 27 ‖ Cant. 1. 2 *l* | 7. 13 Ecclus. 24. 15 ‖ S. John 12. 3 ‖ 2 Cor. 2. 15.

274. *That we ought to follow good examples, and that the lives of the Saints are our incitements to well-doing.*

Gen. 18. 6 ‖ Ex. 12. 11 | 13. 19 | 25. 30, 38 26. 14 | 28. 9 ‖ Deut. 32. 7 ‖ Job 6. 19 | 8. 8 10. 17 ‖ Ps. 104. 13 *l* ‖ Prov. 5. 16 ‖ Jer. 6. 17 38. 12 ‖ 1 Macc. 2. 51 ‖ S. Matt. 5. 16 | 21. 7 Philip. 4. 5.

275. *That we are not to imitate evil examples; or, against those who set evil examples.*

2 Sam. 16. 13 ‖ Ps. 119. 100 ‖ Prov. 1. 17 Jer 7. 30.

276. *That understanding is deservedly taken away from those who do evil works.*

Gen. 11. 2 | 14. 11 | 19. 11 ‖ Deut. 28. 23 | 34. 7 Judg. 7. 5 ‖ Job 5. 13 | 12. 24 | 19. 8 | 20. 14 | 24. 13 28. 13 ‖ Ps. 78. 45 | 105. 29 ‖ Prov. 27. 7 ‖ Is. 1. 6 6. 9 | 19. 14 | 28. 7 | 29. 10, 14 *l* | 59. 2, 9 | 63. 17 Jer. 2. 16 ‖ 8. 8 | 15. 9 | 31. 30 | 33. 5 | 39. 7 Lam. 3. 16 ‖ Wis. 1. 3 ‖ Ecclus. 15. 7 ‖ Amos 4. 5 Mic. 3. 5, 6 ‖ Zeph. 1. 6.

277. *That a curse is given to those who do ill.*

Gen. 3. 17 *l* | 4. 11 | 9. 25 | 49. 4 ‖ Num. 23. 11 Deut. 27. 15 to the end | 28. 15 to end ‖ 2 Kings 2. 24 Job 24. 18 ‖ Jer. 29. 22 | 48. 10 ‖ S. Matt. 21. 19 S. Mark 11. 14 ‖ Acts 5. 4, 5 ‖ Heb. 6. 8 ‖ Rev. 22. 18.

278. *Of scandals.*

Esth. 1. 16 ‖ Ps. 119. 161, 165 ‖ Jer. 7. 30 S. Matt. 17. 27 | 18. 6, 10 ‖ S. Mark 9. 43 | 14. 27 S. Luke 15. 25 ‖ 1 Cor. 1. 22 ‖ Gal. 5. 11 ‖ Rev. 2. 24.

Fourth Part.

279. *Against evil thoughts; or, the sins of the heart.*

Josh. 5. 15 ‖ 1 Sam. 1. 18 ‖ Prov. 6. 14 ‖ 26. 25 Ecclus. 12. 16.

280. *Of the malice and depth of the heart.*

Job 28. 11 ‖ Is. 29. 15 ‖ Jer. 12. 2 *l* ‖ Dan. 2. 22 S. Matt. 7. 16 | 15. 8.

281. *Of simplicity and its commendation.*

Gen. 20. 5 *l* | 25. 27 *l* ‖ Deut. 1. 39 *m* ‖ 1 Chron. 27. 17 *m* ‖ Job 1. 1 *m* | 31. 6 | 33. 3 ‖ Prov. 2. 21 10. 9 | 11. 3, 5, 20 | 19. 1, 27 | 28. 6, 18 ‖ Wis. 1. 1 *l* 1 Macc. 2. 60 ‖ S. Matt. 10. 16 *l* ‖ Rom. 12. 8 *m* 16. 19 *l* ‖ 2 Cor. 1. 12 | 8. 2 | 11. 3.

282. *Of good thoughts and meditations.*

Gen. 24. 63 ‖ Job 35. 5 ‖ Ps. 1. 2 *l* | 13. 2 15. 2 *l* | 16. 9 | 63. 7 | 77. 3, 5 | 119. 16, 24, 48, 92, 97, 99 ‖ Prov. 15. 28 | 21. 5 | 27. 11 ‖ Is. 21. 7 *l* 43. 27 ‖ Jer. 31. 21 ‖ Hab. 2. 1 ‖ Job 4. 5 Wis. 6. 16 | 8. 9 | 9. 15 ‖ Ecclus. 3. 21 | 6. 37 14. 21 | 17. 5 | 27. 11 | 31. 1 | 44. 6.

283. *Of the memory of our birth, human fragility, and death.*

Gen. 3. 16, 19 | 16. 8 | 18. 27 ‖ 1 Sam. 5. 4 Job 10. 9 ‖ Prov. 31. 30 ‖ Eccles. 2. 11, 16, 23 3. 19 | 6. 7 | 7. 2 | 11. 8 | 12. 1 ‖ Is. 9. 14 | 11. 4 *l* 13. 20 *l* | 19. 15 | 43. 5 ‖ Lam. 1. 9 ‖ Zech. 8. 7 Ecclus. 7. 36 | 38. 22 | 40. 1 | 41. 1.

284. *Of our keeping in remembrance the shortness and misery of human life; and death.*

Gen. 3. 16, 19 | 16. 8 | 18. 27 ‖ 1 Sam. 5. 4 Job 10. 9 | 14. 10 ‖ Prov. 31. 30 ‖ Eccles. 2. 11, 16, 23 3. 19 | 6. 7 | 7. 2 | 11. 8 | 12. 1, 5 *l* ‖ Is. 9. 14 11. 4 *m* | 13. 20 | 19. 15 ‖ Jer. 2. 25 *l* ‖ Ecclus. 7. 36 38. 22 | 40. 1 | 41. 1.

285. *That we should remember our sins and the benefits of* God.

Ex. 13. 3, 16 ‖ Deut. 6. 9, 20, 21 | 7. 18 | 8. 2, 11, 15 | 9. 7 | 11. 18 | 31. 19 ‖ Ps. 51. 3 ‖ Is. 43. 26 Ezek. 16. 61.

286. *Of the knowledge of sin.*

Jer. 15. 19 | 51. 6 ‖ Nah. 3. 7 ‖ Eph. 5. 13.

287. *That we ought frequently to call to recollection our sins that we may the better confess them.*

Gen. 1. 9 | 27. 9 | 38. 17 ‖ Ex. 12. 8, 34 ‖ Lev. 5. 8 Num. 16. 39 ‖ Deut. 9. 7 ‖ Judg. 1. 33 *m* | 13. 9 1 Sam. 17. 48, 51 ‖ Job 10. 2 | 13. 23 ‖ Ps. 33. 7 Prov. 20. 30 | 31. 14 ‖ Is. 38. 15, 21 | 43. 3 Jer. 2. 23 ‖ Lam. 3. 40 ‖ Ezek. 16. 61 ‖ Hos. 11. 4 Amos 9. 11 ‖ Judith 13. 6 ‖ 1 Macc. 3. 12 ‖ S. Luke 13. 8.

288. *That we ought to keep in memory the examples of the Saints, to the end that we may imitate them.*

Ex. 12. 11 | 25. 23 ‖ Lev. 1. 7 ‖ Cant. 3. 9 | 8. 9 *l* Jer. 38. 11 ‖ S. Matt. 11. 29 ‖ S. John 13. 13 1 Cor. 11. 1.

289. *That we ought to keep* God *in our memory and in our thoughts; or, against those who forget* God.

Gen. 40. 23 ‖ Deut. 4. 9 | 11. 18 | 31. 19 32. 18, 46 ‖ Josh. 1. 8 ‖ Prov. 3. 6 ‖ Cant. 8. 6 Jer. 2. 32 ‖ Wis. 6. 16.

290. *That we must purge our affections and understanding from sin, to the end that we may obtain the grace of meditation; and of that holiness, without which no man shall see* GOD.

Gen. 7. 2 | 15. 11 ‖ Ex. 8. 12, 31 | 17. 13 | 19. 10
Lev. 11. 43 | 13. 44 | 14. 2, 8 | 17. 15 | 21. 17
Num. 19. 9 | 21. 9 | 28. 2 ‖ Josh. 3. 16 | 5. 15
2 Kings 4. 3 | 5. 14 Job 9. 30 | 14. 4 | 25. 5
39. 5 ‖ Ps. 51. 10 | 78. 56 | 119. 1 ‖ Prov. 4. 23
16. 17 *l* | 22. 11 | 25. 4 | 27. 18 *f* ‖ Eccles. 10. 1
Cant. 3. 7 | 4. 7 ‖ Is. 1. 16 | 6. 6 | 28. 9 | 40. 3
49. 9 | 52. 2, 11 | 57. 14 *l* | 58. 6, 9 *l* | 62. 10
Jer. 2. 18 | 4. 1, 3, 11, 14 | 7. 11 | 17. 21 ‖ Mal. 3. 2
Wis. 1. 5 | 8. 20 ‖ Ecclus. 34. 4 ‖ S. Matt. 3. 12
5. 8 | 8. 2 | 15. 8 | 21. 12 ‖ S. Luke 5. 2 *l* | 11. 34
S. John 2. 15 | 9. 7 | 13. 10 ‖ Acts 15. 9 ‖ 1 Cor. 5. 7
Eph. 4. 23 ‖ Rev. 21. 18 *l*.

291. *That in solitude we have leisure for the study of wisdom and for meditation.*

Gen. 12. 1 | 16. 7 | 18. 1 | 24. 63 ‖ Ex. 2. 15 *m*
3. 1 | 8. 27 | 16. 23 | 24. 2 | Job 3. 13 | 4. 13
39. 5 ‖ Ps. 46. 10 *f* | 55. 6. 7 | 102. 6 ‖ Cant. 3. 11
Is. 2. 10 | 21. 8 | 26. 20 | 32. 2 | 40. 3 | 41. 19
Jer. 15. 17 | 39. 5 | 48. 28 *m* ‖ Lam. 3. 26 ‖ Ezek. 3. 22 ‖ Dan. 6. 10 ‖ Hos. 2. 14 ‖ Wis. 8. 16 | 9. 15
1 Macc. 2. 28 ‖ S. Matt. 4. 1 | 6. 24 | 9. 25. | 17. 1
S. Mark 2. 3 | 3. 13, 19 *l* | 5. 40 | 6. 31 | 7. 33
S. Luke 4. 1, 42 | 5. 16 | 6. 12 | 9. 18 | 19. 4
2 Tim. 2. 4 ‖ Heb. 13. 11.

292. *That they who set their affections on the things which can be seen, neglect those which cannot be seen, and the contrary.*

Ps. 92. 6 ‖ Ecclus. 27. 1 *l* ‖ S. Luke 12. 36
S. John 9. 39 ‖ 1 Cor. 2. 14.

293. *Of those that have too many occupations.*

Nah. 3. 16 ‖ Ecclus. 5. 8 | 11. 10 | 24. 26 34. 9 | 38, 25 ‖ 2 Tim. 2. 4.

294. *Of the continual meditation of wisdom and of the law of* God.

Gen. 1. 17 | 25. 11 ‖ Ex. 2. 15 | 16. 16 | 25. 14 Deut. 6. 6 | 8. 3 ‖ 11. 18 | 17. 18 ‖ Josh. 1. 8 2 Chron. 31. 4 ‖ Neh. 8. 2 ‖ Job 33. 14 ‖ Ps. 119. 2, 18, 34, 46, 73 ‖ Prov. 3. 3 | 6. 21 | 7. 3 Cant. 5. 12 ‖ Is. 21. 8 ‖ Jer. 15. 16 ‖ Ezek. 3. 1 Ecclus. 6. 37 | 11. 20 | 14. 20 | 32. 15*f* | 39. 1 S. John 5. 39 ‖ 1 Tim. 4. 13.

295. *That we ought to take pleasure in the seeking out and the hearing wisdom.*

Prov. 1. 5 | 8. 34 | 18. 13 | 19. 27 ‖ Is. 1. 17*f* 5. 13*f* | 11. 9*l* | 27. 11 | 30. 8 | 42. 18 | 50. 4 Jer. 6. 16 Wis. 6. 14 ‖ Ecclus. 3. 29 | 6. 36 | 8. 9 18. 19*f* ‖ Bar. 3. 14, 27 ‖ S. Matt. 12. 41 ‖ S. Luke 11. 32 ‖ Acts 8. 30 ‖ S. James 1. 19.

296. *That wisdom is to be sought, not only by reading and meditation, but by prayer and good works.*

1 Kings 3. 9 " Ps. 43. 3 | 119. 18 ‖ Wis. 8. 21 Ecclus. 1. 26 | 51. 18 ‖ S. James 1. 5.

297. *That this grace is principally obtained by loving* God.

Wis. 6. 13 ‖ Ecclus. 1. 10 | 24. 19 ‖ S. John 14. 21.

298. *That the grace of obtaining wisdom is not acquired by human virtue, but is given by* God.

Job 28. 21 | 32. 8 | 36. 26 | 37. 23 ‖ Eccles. 7. 24 8. 17 Wis. 9. 14 " Ecclus. 6. 33 ‖ S. Matt. 7. 11 1 Cor. 12. 7.

(95)

299. *Of the greatness of the consolation of Divine wisdom, or of Holy Scripture; and that, in troubles whether external or internal.*
Gen. 22. 1 | 42. 7, 24 | 43. 27 | 45. 1 || Ex. 1. 12 Job. 2. 3, 10 | 11. 14 | 22. 23 | Ps. 18. 35 *l* | 90. 15 121. 7 || Jer. 30. 11, 17 || Tob. 4. 21 || Ecclus. 2. 1 27. 5 | 1 Macc. 4. 30 || 2 Macc. 6. 13 || S. John 16. 20 || Acts 14. 24 || Rom. 6. 5 || 8. 18. 35 | 14 7 15. 4 || 1 Cor. 10. 13 | 11. 32 | 2 Cor. 4. 16 | 5. 1 6. 4 | 8. 2 | 12. 9 Heb. 11. 14 | 12. 3, 11 | 13. 5 *l* 1 S. Pet. 2. 19, 21 | 4. 12 | 5. 10 || Rev. 1. 9 2. 10, 17 | 3. 5, 11 | 7. 3, 14 | 12. 7 | 21. 7.

300. *Of the benefit to be derived from the contemplation of wisdom; which sanctifies, blesses, and gives joy and strength.*
Gen. 2. 5 *m*, 10 | 26. 19 || Ex. 12. 34 | 16. 15 *l* 2 Kings 4. 5 || Job 28. 17 || Ps. 104. 10 || Prov. 4. 7 9. 1 | 15. 30 | 24. 3 | 27. 11 || Eccles. 7. 19 | 9. 18 11. 7 || Is. 41. 18 | 58. 12 || Wis. 6. 17 | 7. 27 8. 7, 16 | 9. 6, 20 | 16. 20 || Ecclus 4. 12, 18 | 6. 18 15. 3 | 24. 7 | 40. 20 || 51. 20, 28 || S. Luke 10. 42 11. 34 | S. John 4, 13 | 7. 38 || 1 Cor. 2. 6 | Col. 1. 9 || Heb. 5. 14.

301. *Against the will of this world.*
Job. 5. 13 *f* || Prov. 26. 12 || Is. 33. 18 || Jer. 49. 7 || 1 Cor. 1. 19 | 3. 19.

302. *That there is no wisdom where sin reigns.*
Gen. 37. 20 *m* || Ex. 9. 18 | 10. 13 || Num. 21. 5 24. 3 | 1 Sam. 8. 1 || 1 Kings 11. 3 || Job. 20. 14 Ps. 74. 10, 16 | 117. 18, 27 || Is. 3. 1 | 8. 6 | 13. 9 58. 7 || Ezek. 7. 19 || Joel. 1. 4, 17 || Hag. 1. 4.

303. *Against foolish men; or, of folly.*
1 Sam. 25. 25 || Job. 5. 2 | Ps. 92. 6 | Prov. 10. 1 12. 16 | 15. 2 *l* | 26. 4 | 29. 11 || Eccles. 7. 7 Is. 32. 4, 6 || Ecclus. 22. 7, 18 | 33. 5 || S. Matt. 5. 13 | 25. 3.

304. *That the Egyptians are to be spoiled, in order that the Hebrews may be enriched.*

Ex. 2. 9 | 11. 2 | 18. 24 || Deut. 20. 20 || 2 Sam. 8. 7 || Zech. 6. 11 || 1 Macc. 3. 12 || Acts 22. 3.

305. *Against those who give too much attention to worldly knowledge.*

Gen. 54. 29 | 26. 18, 24 || Ex. 7. 12 | 34. 30 Deut. 7. 12 | 31. 11 || Judg. 12. 6 || 1 Sam. 17, 39 2 Sam. 3. 27 || 2 Kings 1. 3 | 5. 12 | 22. 11 2 Chron. 17. 9 || Neh. 13. 23 || Ps. 119. 2 | 141. 7 Prov. 18. 1 | 20. 17 || Is. 22. 10 | 29. 4 | 55. 2 Jer. 2. 13, 18 | 8. 19 *m*, 22 | 9. 5 || Ezek. 3. 5 S. Matt. 12. 42 || S. Luke 8. 43 || S. John 3. 31 8. 47 | 1 Cor. 1. 20 || S. James 3. 15 || 1 S. John 2. 19 | 4. 5.

306. *Of counsel.*

Gen. 27. 8 | 28. 2 || Ex. 18. 14 || Prov. 20. 18 27. 9 || Ecclus. 32. 18, 19 || 1 Macc. 2. 49.

307. *Against those who despise, or, who do not seek for wholesome counsel.*

1 Sam. 30. 8 || 1 Kings 12. 13 || 2 Chron. 25. 17 Job 18. 7 || Prov. 1. 31 | 8. 12, 14 | 12. 15 *l*, 20 *l* 13. 10 *l*, 16 | 15. 22 | 19. 20 | 24. 6 | 25. 9 | 31. 13 Tob. 4. 19 || Ecclus. 6. 6 | 18. 7 | 11. 29 | 19. 8 37. 16 || Macc. 2. 65 | 5. 66.

308. *Against the counsels of wicked men.*

Job 5. 12, 13 | 12. 17 | 18. 7 || Ps. 9. 16 | 21. 11 33. 10 | 94. 11 || Is. 42. 14 | 44. 25 | 47. 13 59. 4, 5, 7 || S. John 11. 47 || 1 Cor. 1. 19 | 3. 19.

309. *Against those who keep back the truth when they are called to counsel.*

Gen. 37. 21 || 1 Kings 22. 8 || Judith 5. 5 S. Matt. 27. 24 || S. Luke 23. 4 || S. John 19. 6 *l* Acts 5. 34, 38 | 18. 6 | 23. 9.

(97)

310. *That the truth is sometimes to be kept back.*

Gen. 12. 13 | 20. 2 ‖ Prov. 20. 19 | 25. 2 ‖ Tob. 12. 7.

311. *Of prayer, and its efficacy.*

Ex. 8. 9 | 14. 16 | 32. 11 ‖ Num. 11. 2 | 12. 13 16. 31 ‖ Josh. 10. 13 | 1 Sam. 1. 15, 27 ‖ 7. 8 12. 23 | 1 Kings 3. 9 | 17. 1, 21 | 18. 38 ‖ 2 Kings 4. 34 | 20. 10 | 2 Chron. 20. 3 | 30. 1, 20 | Ezra 10. 1 Ps. 4. 1 | 42. 2 | 54. 2 | 119. 145 | 141. 2 | 142. 2 Is. 58. 12 *l* | Dan. 2. 18 | 6. 10 | Zech. 10. 1 Tob. 3. 1, 11 | 12. 8 | Judith 4. 12 | 6. 18, 21 *l* 9. 1 | 13. 7 | Wis. 18. 22 ‖ Eccles. 2. 10 *l* | 18. 22 35. 17 | 37. 15 | 51. 19 ‖ Bar. 2. 14 ‖ Sus. 42 2 Macc. 6. 30 | 15. 27 | S. Matt. 5. 44 | 6. 5, 9 7. 7 | 14. 23 *m* | 17. 20 | S. Luke 6. 12 | 18. 1 21. 36 | 22. 33 | 23. 34 | Acts 1. 14 | 7. 59 9. 3, 4, 40 | 10. 4 ‖ Rom. 1. 9 | 12. 13 | Col. 4. 2 1 Thess. 5. 17 ‖ 1 Tim. 2. 1 ‖ S. James 1. 5 5. 15, 16 *l*.

312. *That we must first prepare our life, if we would have our prayers efficacious.*

Ps. 145. 19 ‖ Is. 38. 2 | 58. 9 ‖ Jon. 3. 5 Ecclus. 18. 23 | 35. 1, 17 *f* | 38. 10.

313. *That the thoughts of this world ought to be banished when we pray.*

Gen. 15. 11 ‖ S. Matt. 6. 6 | 14. 23 | S. Mark 6. 46 ‖ S. Luke 5. 16, 18 | S. John 2. 15.

314. *What we ought to pray for.*

Josh. 15. 19 ‖ Ruth 4. 11 | Prov. 30. 7 | Tob. 4. 19 Ecclus. 38. 9 ‖ S. Matt. 6. 33 | 24. 20 | 26. 44 S. Mark 14. 39 ‖ S. Luke 6. 12 | 21. 36 ‖ S. John 16. 34 ‖ Rom. 8. 26 ‖ 1 Cor. 1. 2 ‖ 1 Thess. 5. 17 S. James 1. 5.

H

315. *That we must add tears to our prayers.*

1 Sam. 1. 10 ‖ Ps. 102. 9 ‖ Is. 38. 5 ‖ Tob. 3. 10, 11
12. 8.

316. *Of perseverance in prayer.*

2 Chron. 20. 3 ‖ Judith 4. 9, 13 ‖ S. Luke 6. 12 *l*
18. 1 ‖ Eph. 6. 18 ‖ Col. 4. 2 ‖ 1 Thess. 5. 17
1 Tim. 2. 8 ‖ S. James 5. 16 *l*.

317. *That it is advantageous to pray for others.*

Ex. 8. 9, 29 | 10. 17 | 17. 11 | 106. 23 ‖ S. Matt.
15. 23 ‖ S. Luke 4. 38 *l* ‖ Eph. 6. 18, 19 ‖ S. James
5. 14, 16, 17.

318. *That GOD does not regard the supplications of sinners.*

Judg. 2. 18 *l* | 10. 10, 13 ‖ Job 8. 13 *l* ‖ Prov.
1. 27 | 15. 29 | 21. 31 | 28. 9 ‖ Is. 1. 15 ‖ Jer. 11. 11 *l*
Ezek. 7. 25 | 8. 18 ‖ Hos. 5. 6 ‖ Mic. 3. 4 ‖ Ecclus.
34. 26 ‖ S. Matt. 7. 21 ‖ S. James 4. 2.

319. *That GOD answers speedily.*

Gen. 27. 27 ‖ 2 Sam. 12. 13 ‖ Ps. 10. 19 | 32. 5
33. 17 | 34. 17 ‖ Is. 65. 24 ‖ Wis. 6. 13 ‖ S. Luke
15. 22.

320. *That GOD gives more than we ask.*

1 Kings 3. 13 ‖ S. Matt. 6. 33 | 9. 2 ‖ S. Luke
1. 63 ‖ 2 Cor. 9. 10.

321. *That the knowledge of GOD is to be sought for
earnestly and indefatigably.*

Gen. 32. 30 ‖ Ex. 33. 18 ‖ Job 11. 15 | 29. 39
Ps. 5. 3 | 16. 9 | 24. 6 | 25. 14 | 27. 5 | 31. 17
32. 9 | 34. 5, 8 | 36. 8 | 42. 2 | 43. 4 | 46. 10 | 77. 5
80. 1 *l*, 4 | 84. 2, 5 | 86. 3 | 105. 4 | 143. 8 ‖ Is. 32. 4
Jer. 51, 50 *l* ‖ 2 Cor. 3. 18 ‖ Philip 3. 20 ‖ Heb.
11. 27.

322. *That we are not to be wise above that which is written; or, of the uninvestigable excellency of* God.
Ex. 12. 9, 46 *l* | 19. 12 *l* ‖ Job 5. 13 | 9. 2 | 11. 2, 7 | 26. 14 | 36. 23, 26 | 37. 24 ‖ Ps. 35. 10 | 64. 6 | 77. 3 ‖ Prov. 14. 6 | 22. 28 | 23. 1 | 25. 16 | 30. 33 | Eccles. 1. 13 | 2. 26 | 3. 10 | 7. 16 | 20. 4 | 8. 17 | 10. 15 ‖ Cant. 6. 5 ‖ Is. 33. 18 | 38. 14 | 40. 28 *l* | 43. 26 | 45. 14 | 47. 10, 13 | 53. 8 ‖ Jer. 49. 7 | Ezek. 7. 19 ‖ Amos 1. 3 ‖ Rom. 1. 22 | 12. 3 | 1 Cor. 1. 19 | 2. 14.

323. *Of desires and longings.*
Gen. 49. 26 ‖ Job 3. 24 | 31. 35 | 42. 2, 3 | Is. 26. 9 | 41. 17 | 53. 2 ‖ Philip 1. 23.

324. *Of the praise of* God.
Ps. 22. 25 | 34. 1 | 92. 1 | 95. 1, &c. ‖ Is. 21. 12 | 26. 9, 19 | 38. 20 | 43. 21 | 48. 9 ‖ Hos. 14. 2 *l* | Rev. 15. 3.

325. *Against the ingratitude of man for the benefits of* God.
Deut. 32. 15 ‖ 1 Sam. 25. 38 ‖ 2 Chron. 24. 22 | Esth. 6. 3 ‖ Eccles. 9. 15 ‖ Jer. 5. 7, 27 ‖ Hos. 2. 8 | 7. 15 | 13. 6 ‖ Mic. 7. 1 ‖ S. Matt. 18. 32 ‖ S. Luke 17. 17.

326. *Of attention in prayer; and against those who sing undevoutly and irreverently, and who cut short the words of the* Lord.
Gen. 23. 1 ‖ Ps. 2. 11 | 5. 1 | 9. 2, 11 | 33. 3 | 35. 28 | 37. 31 | 45. 2 | 47. 7 | 71. 7, 22 | 92. 1 | 119. 54 | 130. 2 | 138. 1 *l* | 147. 1 ‖ Neh. 1. 11 *f* | 8. 8 ‖ Is. 29. 13 ‖ Jer. 48. 10 *f* ‖ Ecclus. 39. 35 | S. Matt. 15. 8 ‖ S. Luke 9. 29 ‖ Eph. 6. 18 | 1 S. Pet. 4. 7 | 5. 8.

327. *Against profane songs.*
Ex. 32. 18 *l* ‖ Amos 5. 23 | 6. 5.

328. *That on Sundays, and other festivals, we are not to indulge in idleness, but are to labour in the praise of* GOD, *and prayer and preaching.*

Ex. 20. 8 | 23. 27 ‖ Is. 56. 2 ‖ Jer. 17. 21 Lam. 1. 7 *l* ‖ Acts 13. 27 | 20. 7 ‖ 1 Cor. 16. 2.

FIFTH BOOK.

First Part.

329. *Of manna and the Bread of Life.*

Ex. 16. 35 | 25. 30 | 26. 26 ' Josh. 1. 7 | 5. 12
1 Sam. 21. 4   Ps. 68. 9 | 78. 26 ‖ Is. 3. 7
Ezek. 37. 12 | S. Matt. 26. 26 ‖ S. Mark 6. 41
14. 22 ‖ S. Luke 22. 19 ‖ S. John 6. 50, 51 ‖ S. James
5. 17.

330. *What prelates are to be elected, and how.*

Gen. 14. 18 | 30. 37 | 33. 12 | 41. 39 ‖ Ex. 12. 11
18. 21 | 26. 1 | 28. 1 | 31. 2 ' Lev. 19. 2 ‖ Num.
11. 16 | 27. 16   Deut. 1. 13 | 17. 15 | 33. 9
Judg. 9. 8 ' 1 Sam. 9. 2 | 14. 52 | 16. 7 ‖ 2 Kings
4. 29 | Ps. 2. 6 | 110. 4 , Is. 3. 6 | 22. 20 | 44. 28
Jer. 3. 15   Wis. 18. 24 ‖ 1 Macc. 10. 19   S. Matt.
14. 19 | 10. 5 | 24. 45   S. Luke 15. 22 ' S. John
15. 16 ‖ Acts 1. 24 | 13. 2 ‖ 1 Tim. 3. 2 ‖ Tit. 1. 7
Heb. 5. 4.

331. *Against those who thrust themselves into the office of a Bishop; or, by what signs the ambitious are distinguished.*

Ex. 4. 10 ‖ Judg. 6. 15 | 9. 8 ‖ 1 Sam. 10. 21
2 Sam. 15. 2 ‖ 1 Kings 3. 7   Prov. 29. 2 ‖ Is. 3. 7
Jer. 1. 6 | 5. 4 | 1 Macc. 7. 21 ‖ 2 Macc. 4. 7
S. Matt. 20. 20 | 22. 11 ' S. John 6. 15 ‖ Acts 8. 18
Heb. 5. 4 | 12. 2.

332. *That a prelate or a preacher ought to excel others in his life and his works.*

Deut. 17. 15 ‖ Josh. 3. 6 *l* ‖ 1 Sam. 9. 2 ‖ S. John
10. 4 ‖ Heb. 5. 1.

333. *That every prelate ought to be a preacher.*

2 Chron. 17. 9 | Ps. 2. 6 | Jer. 1. 10.

334. *That a prelate or a preacher ought to have the Word of God in his heart.*

Ezra 9. 3 | 10. 1 | Job 39. 30 | Ps. 119. 20, 97, 103 | Prov. 10. 31 | 15. 14 | 16. 23 | 21. 1 | Is. 9. 3 | 33. 7 | Jer. 51. 8 | Ezek. 3. 15 | 1 Macc. 1. 27 | S. John 5. 35 | 2 Cor. 6. 11 | 11. 29 | Gal. 4. 9 | Rev. 12. 1.

335. *That a prelate or a preacher should show forth his knowledge by his words.*

Gen. 41. 39 | 47. 6 | Ex. 18. 19 | 24. 14 | Lev. 4. 3 | Deut. 17, 8, 18 | 1 Sam. 5. 1 | 13. 19 | Ezra 7. 10 | Ps. 32. 9 | 105. 21 | 119. 73 | Eccles. 10. 5 | Is. 28. 7 | 56. 10 | Lam. 1. 6 | Ezek. 2. 9 | Hag. 2. 11 | Zech. 11. 17 | Mal. 2. 7 | Ecclus. 5. 12 | S. Matt. 24. 25 || S. John 6. 13 | Eph. 4. 11 | 1 Tim. 3. 2 | 2 Tim. 3. 14 | Tit. 1. 7 || 1 S. Pet. 3. 15.

336. *Of pastoral care.*

Gen. 30. 27 | 31. 38 | Ex. 32. 11, 32 | Num. 11. 12 | 27. 16 || Deut. 9. 25 | Job 39. 27 | Prov. 6. 1 | 27. 23 || Cant. 7. 12 | Is. 21. 8 | 40. 11 | 62. 6 | Ezek. 34. 2, 10, 11 | Hab. 2. 2 | Wis. 18. 21 | Ecclus. 29. 14 | 37. 26 | 1 Macc. 3. 4, 8 | 5. 53 | S. Matt. 4. 23 | S. Luke 2. 8 | 4. 43 | S. John 10. 2 | Acts 20. 31 | 1 Cor. 9. 20, 22 | 2 Cor. 11. 28 | Heb. 11. 37 | 13. 7 || 1 S. Pet. 5. 2 | Rev. 1. 12, 13.

337. *Of the affection of prelates to those over whom they are set.*

Ex. 32. 31 || Num. 16. 26, 45 | 27. 16 || Deut. 9. 18, 25 || Josh. 7. 6, 8 | 1 Sam. 12. 23 | 15. 35 | 2 Sam. 24. 17 || Job 39. 14, 15 | Is. 22. 4 | Jer. 4. 31 | 9. 1, 17 | 14. 17 | 18. 20 *l* | Lam. 2. 19 | Bar. 4. 11 | 1 Macc. 2. 7, 12 | 4. 38 | 5. 53 || S. Luke 19. 29.

338. *Of the condescension of prelates.*

Gen. 2. 21 | 33. 13 | 42. 15 || Num. 11. 12 Deut. 1. 31 || 2 Sam. 23. 8 || 2 Kings 4. 32 || Job 39. 1 || Ps. 144. 5 || Prov. 12. 10 || Cant. 5. 5 Is. 40. 11 | 41. 14 | 57. 14 | 63. 9 | 64. 1 || Hos. 11. 3 S. Matt. 23. 2, 4 || S. Luke 5. 37 || S. John 10. 11 Acts 20. 33 | Rom. 14. 1 | 15. 1 || 1 Cor. 1. 25 9. 22 || 1 Thess. 2. 5.

339. *That by the example of a good prelate his people prospers and is saved.*

Gen. 30. 29 | 39. 5 || Judg. 2. 7, 18 | 2 Kings 12. 2 | Ps. 132. 9 | Jer. 31. 14.

340. *That the people suffers for the sins of evil prelates.*

1 Sam. 4. 10 | 28. 19 || 2 Kings 21. 11 || Job 20. 10 21. 17 | 27. 13 || Eccles. 9. 14 Is. 3. 4, 5 | 14. 20 *l* 52. 5 Jer. 7. 17 | 10. 21 | 11. 22 | 12. 9, 10 14. 17, 18 | 15. 4 | 32. 18 *m* Lam. 4. 12, 13 Hos. 7. 1 | 9. 11, 15 || Jon. 1. 12 || Ecclus. 41. 6.

341. *Of the corruption of the people which follows the ill-example of a prelate.*

1 Sam. 4. 18 || 1 Kings 12. 28 || 2 Chron. 33. 9 Esth. 1. 16 Job 12. 15 | 19. 9 | 24. 3 | Prov. 11. 14 14, 4 | 25. 26 Is. 3. 4 | 32. 7 | 42. 20 | 49. 17 52. 5 || Jer. 7. 18, 31 | 12. 10 | 19. 5 | 23. 14 50. 6 || Lam. 1. 6 Ezek. 16. 20 | 34. 5 || Hos. 4. 18 | 5. 1 | 6. 10 | 9. 8 || Joel 2. 31 Mic. 2. 8 Zech. 11. 5 || Mal. 2. 8 || Wis. 4. 6 || Ecclus. 10. 13 *f* 2 Macc. 4. 7.

342. *That the devil endeavours to destroy one prelate more than many of those who are set under him.*

Num. 31. 7. || 1 Sam. 23. 22 | 31. 2 || Ps. 37. 12 S. Luke 23. 31.

343. *Of the punishment and deposition of evil prelates.*

Lev. 10. 1 | 20. 4 ‖ Num. 25. 3 | Judg. 2. 18
9. 23 | 1 Sam. 2. 27 | 13. 13 | 15. 26 | 31. 2 | 2 Sam.
6. 6 | Prov. 20. 16 ‖ Is. 14. 5, 12, 19 | 22. 15, 16
28. 14, 27 | 32. 5 | 34. 2, 5 | Jer. 9. 10 *f* | 23. 2
25. 34 | 51. 23, 25 | Ezek. 6. 2 | 9. 6 | 21. 26
33. 6 | 34. 10 | Hos. 4. 6 | Joel 2. 1 ‖ Amos 6. 1, 8, 11
Zeph. 1. 8 | Zech. 1. 14 | 8. 2 | 10. 3 | 11. 17
Ecclus. 12. 13 | S. Matt. 18. 6 ‖ S. Luke 13. 7.

344. *To what evil things wicked prelates are compared by the* LORD.

Judg. 9. 14 | Job 24. 5 | 39. 16 | Ps. 22. 12
49. 20 | 58. 4 | Is. 1. 22 | 34. 7, 11, 13 | 48. 4
51. 20 | 56. 10 | 59. 11 | Jer. 5. 26 | 6. 30 | Lam.
5. 18 | Ezek. 13. 4 | 22. 18 | Hos. 7. 11, 16
Joel 1. 17 | Amos 4. 1 | Nah. 3. 17 ‖ Zeph. 3. 3
Zech. 9. 3 | 11. 17 | S. Matt. 3. 7 | 23. 27, 33
S. Luke 13. 32 | Acts 23. 3.

345. *That flatterers gain favour with wicked prelates and the good are despised and ridiculed.*

1 Sam. 22. 9 | 2 Sam. 15. 12 | 1 Kings 22. 6, 8. 11
2 Chron. 18. 7 | Esth. 3. 5 | Prov. 29. 12 ‖ Jer.
28. 11.

346. *Against prelates that keep silence when they ought to speak.*

Gen. 24. 33 | 1 Sam. 3. 13 ″ Job 31. 38 ″ Ps. 40. 11
71. 15, 22 | 73. 27 *l* | 78. 7 | 119. 13 | Is. 6. 5
22. 15 | 40. 2 | 58. 1 | 62. 1 | Jer. 31. 6 | 50. 2
Lam. 2. 10 | Ezek. 3. 18 | 20. 4, 49 | 33. 6 | Hos.
8. 1 ‖ Ecclus. 20. 31 ‖ Acts 20. 26 ‖ 2 Tim. 4. 1.

347. *That wicked ecclesiastics are worse than wicked laymen; or, against those that ought to be better and are worse.*

Ex. 6. 12 | 12. 33 | 28. 43 ″ Ps. 132. 6 ‖ Is. 1. 28
23. 4 ‖ Jer. 2. 10 ‖ Ezek. 16. 27 ‖ Hos. 8. 8 ‖ Jon. 1. 6
Mic. 7. 4.

(105)

348. *Against ecclesiastics who say that they ought not to be reproved before laymen.*

Lev. 19. 17 *l*   Neh. 8. 3 ‖ Prov. 10. 17 ‖ Jer. 28. 7 S. Matt. 23. 3 ǀ S. Luke 11. 29 ǀ 12. 1 ǀ 19. 39 20. 45, 46 ‖ 1 Tim. 5. 20.

349. *Against pluralities.*

Gen. 6. 16   Ex. 18. 17   Lev. 20. 14 ‖ Num. 36. 6, 7   Deut. 1. 12 ǀ 17. 17   2 Kings 4. 6 Ps. 25. 15 ǀ 27. 4   Eccles. 4. 10   Is. 4. 1   Jer. 23. 2 Hos. 8. 11 ǀ 10. 1   S. Luke 19. 21   S. John 4. 38 1 Cor. 9. 13 ǀ 12. 17, 28 ‖ Eph. 4. 11 ‖ S. James 3. 1.

350. *That the revenues of the Church are not to be given to relations, but to the poor; and that he who does otherwise is a robber.*

Gen. 50. 21   Lev. 22. 12   Deut. 12. 17 ǀ 23. 24 26. 14 ‖ 1 Sam. 2. 13   2 Kings 5. 16 ǀ 22. 17 2 Chron. 24. 5, 7   Prov. 28. 24   Jer. 7, 11 S. Matt. 21. 13 ‖ S. John 10. 10 ǀ 12. 5.

351. *Against those who will not be subject to others, and thus imitate the devil.*

1 Sam. 15. 22 *l* ‖ Prov. 1. 24 ‖ Is. 14. 13 ǀ 16. 6 Hos. 4. 4 ‖ Eph. 5. 21 ‖ Philip. 2. 3.

Second Part.

352. *Of the zeal of prelates.*

Ex. 32, 19, 26 ‖ Num. 25. 5 ‖ Josh. 1. 6, 7, 9 7. 24 ‖ 1 Sam. 11. 5, 6 ǀ 15. 33 ǀ 17. 26 ‖ 1 Kings 18. 40   2 Kings 10. 16 ‖ Is. 1. 10 ǀ 56. 10 Jer. 20. 9 ‖ Ezek. 16. 3   Judith 9. 2 ǀ Sus. 52, 56 1 Macc. 2. 6, 7 ‖ S. Mark 15. 43 ‖ S. John 2. 14 Acts 5. 3.

353. *That a priest, or any one that is called to rebuke, ought to correct himself before he corrects others.*
  Lev. 1. 15 ‖ Ecclus. 19. 17 ‖ S. Matt. 7. 3 S. John 8. 6 ‖ Gal. 6. 1.

354. *Of the correction which brings favour and friends.*
  Job 20. 3 Prov. 9. 8 | 24. 25 | 25. 12 | 29. 15 Ecclus. 19. 13 | 1 Macc. 9. 69 | 2 Tim. 4. 2.

355. *That correction should be administered with gentleness and in moderation.*
  Prov. 17. 27 Ecclus. 36. 23 ‖ 1 Cor. 9. 22 1 Tim. 5. 1 ‖ 2 Tim. 2. 24 | 4. 2.

356. *That a gentle correction may amend, where severity would harden, an offender.*
  Gen. 3. 9 | 4. 9 | 9. 2 | 19. 16 | Ex. 2. 13 | 21. 28 22. 6 ‖ Prov. 14. 3 | 15. 1, 4 | 17. 27 | 19. 18 Cant. 4. 3 | Hag. 2. 22 Ecclus. 6. 5 | 8. 11 | 11. 7 20. 2 | 27. 9 | 31. 31 ‖ S. Matt. 18. 15 ‖ Gal. 6. 1 Col. 1. 28 | 1 Thess. 5. 12 | 2 Thess. 3. 14 ‖ 1 Tim. 5. 1 | 2. 24 | S. James 3. 13.

357. *That one is corrected by the example of another; or, that a good man profits from the punishment and sudden death of others.*
  Gen. 9. 13 | 11. 7 | 26. 19 | 42. 1 ‖ Ex. 7. 24 13. 9 Num. 16. 37 | Josh. 7. 27 | Judg. 14. 14 1 Sam. 17. 54 2 Sam. 20. 21 ‖ Ps. 9. 4 | 58. 9 60. 4 | 119. 120 | 120. 5 | Prov. 19. 25 | 21. 11 24. 30, 32 | Is. 5. 25 | 19. 17 | 26. 9 | 28. 19 Jer. 8. 2 | 9. 22 | 16. 4 | Mic. 1. 11 | 2. 4 | Nah. 1. 1 | 3. 7 | Zeph. 1. 17 | 2. 15 | 13. 5 ‖ S. Luke 17. 32 ‖ Acts 5. 11 ‖ 1 Cor. 10, 11 ‖ 1 Tim. 5. 20.

358. *That evil prelates may be rebuked by their inferiors, and may be reverently admonished when they are guilty of enormous sins.*
  Neh. 5. 7 | 13. 11 | 25. 12 ‖ Ecclus. 4. 25 48. 7 | S. Matt. 14. 4 ‖ Gal. 2. 11 | 6. 1.

359. *That rebuke ought not to be administered at all times.*

1 Sam. 25. 36 | Prov. 25. 11 | 26. 7 | Ecclus. 8. 1 | 20. 5, 22 | 22. 6 | 31. 31 | 32. 4.

360. *Against those that despise rebuke.*

Gen. 19. 9 | Ex. 2. 14 | 2 Sam. 23. 6 || Prov. 9. 8 | 10. 17 | 12. 1 | 13. 10 | 15. 10, 32 | 19. 29 | 23. 9 | 21. 1 | 29. 19 | Eccles. 1. 15 | Is. 29. 21 || Jer. 5. 3 | Amos 7. 16 | Mic. 7. 4 | Zeph. 3. 2 | Wis. 12. 26 | Ecclus. 8. 1 | 19. 5 | 21. 6, 12 | 32. 17.

361. *Of the severe correction that is to be administered to the hardened.*

Gen. 34. 30 | 1 Kings 14. 6 || Job 38. 2 | Is. 1. 10, 23 | 22. 15 | 28. 14 | 49. 2 | 56. 10 | 57. 3 | Mic. 5. 1 | Ecclus. 4. 27 || S. Matt. 3. 7 | 12. 39 | 15. 7 | 16. 4 | 17. 17 | 23. 33 || S. Luke 3. 7 | Acts 7. 51 | 14. 10 | 23. 3 | 1 Cor. 4. 21 | Gal. 2. 11 | 1 Tim. 5. 20 | Tit. 1. 13.

362. *That the wicked hate those that correct them.*

Ex. 2. 14 || 1 Kings 18. 17 | 20. 43 | 22. 8 | Job 30. 1 | Prov. 9. 7, 8 | 13. 1 *l* | 15. 12, 32 *f* | 17. 10 | 23. 9 | 27. 22 | 29. 1 | Is. 30. 10 | Jer. 20. 2, 8 | 26. 11 | 38. 4 || Lam. 3. 14 | Amos 5. 10 | 7. 10 | Judith 5. 22 | 6. 1. 13 | Wis. 2. 15 || Ecclus. 6. 20 | 19. 11 | 22. 7 | 32. 17 || S. Matt. 27. 63 | S. Mark 6. 20 | 14. 64 || S. Luke 7. 33 | S. John 8. 40 | 10. 31 | 12. 10 | 18. 22 | Acts 5. 33 | 7. 54 | 16. 19 || Rev. 11. 10.

363. *Against those who excuse their sins; or, who justify themselves.*

Gen. 3. 7, 12 | 4. 9 | 18. 15 || 1 Sam. 15. 20 | 1 Kings 8. 46 || Job 4. 18 | 9. 20 | 25. 5 || Ps. 141. 4 | Eccles. 7. 20 || Is. 13. 22 | 34. 13 | 64. 6 | Jer. 2. 23 | Ecclus. 7. 5 || 1 Cor. 4. 4 || S. James 3. 6 | 1 S. John 1. 10.

364. *Against those, who, through the fear of this world, do ill, or neglect to do well.*
Ps. 14. 5 ‖ Prov. 22. 13 " Jer. 38. 19 | Wis. 17. 10 S. Mark 6. 26 | 15. 15 ‖ S. Luke 12. 9 ‖ S. John 13. 42 ‖ Rom. 12. 2.

365. *That the outward demeanour of the body is a sign of the disposition of the soul.*
Neh. 2. 2   Prov. 17. 22 2 Macc. 3. 16 ‖ S. Luke 9. 29.

366. *Of consolation: or of one that consoles others.*
Gen. 40. 7 | 45. 5 ‖ 1 Chron. 28. 20 " Job. 2. 11   16. 5 | 42. 11 ‖ Ps. 94. 19   Is. 35. 4 | 40. 1 | 49. 13   50. 10 | 51. 12 | 60. 1 | 61. 2 | 66. 10   Tobit 4. 21   5. 20 | 12. 17 | 13. 5 ‖ Bar. 4. 5 " S. Matt. 28. 5   S. Luke 12. 32 | 22. 43   S. John 20. 15   Acts 27. 25   2 Cor. 1. 3 | 2. 7   1 Thess. 4. 18.

367. *Of instructing others.*
Job 4. 3   Prov. 16. 22 | 31. 8, 26 ‖ Eccles. 12. 9   Dan. 11, 33 | 12. 3   Ecclus. 21. 16 | 24. 25 | 37. 23   S. Matt. 5. 19 | 28. 19   1 Cor. 14. 3   Col. 3. 16   1 Tim. 4. 12   Heb. 13. 7.

368. *Of expounding the Scriptures.*
Ezra 7. 10 " Job 28. 11 ‖ Prov. 11, 26 ‖ 12. 8   Ecclus. 24. 29 | 39. 1 | 44. 3.

369. *Of preaching the Gospel.*
Ps. 68. 11 | 71. 16 | 73. 27 *l* | 119. 13 ‖ Is. 40. 9   41. 27 | 48. 20 ‖ Nah. 1. 15 ‖ S. Matt. 11. 5   S. Mark 16. 15 | S. Luke 7. 22.

370. *That a prelate or a preacher ought first to learn before they teach.*
Job 4. 20 | 36. 11 " Ps. 2. 10 ‖ Prov. 1. 5 | 8. 34   18. 13 | 19. 27   Is. 1. 17 | 5. 13 | 11. 9 | 27. 11 *m*   30. 8 | 42. 18 | 50. 4 *l* ‖ Jer. 6. 16 | 22. 20 ‖ Hos. 4. 6, 12 ‖ Zech. 7. 11   Wis. 6. 14 ‖ Ecclus. 3. 29   6. 36 | 8. 9 | 11. 8 " 18. 17 | 32. 8 ‖ Bar. 3. 14, 28   S. Matt. 6. 33 | 12. 42 ‖ S. Luke 2. 46 | 11. 31   Acts 8. 30 ‖ S. James 1. 19.

371. *Of the mission of prelates or of preachers.*

Gen. 8. 8 ‖ Ex. 3. 10 ‖ Num. 13. 2 ‖ Deut. 1. 22 Josh. 2. 1 ‖ Prov. 5. 15 ‖ Is. 55. 11 ‖ Jer. 1. 7 Ezek. 2. 3 | 3. 5   Mic. 6. 3   Mal. 3. 1 ‖ S. Matt. 10. 16 ‖ S. Mark 16. 15 ‖ S. Luke 1. 26 | 10. 1 Rom. 10. 15.

372. *That none, except he be called by* GOD, *should dare to be a prelate.*

Num. 10. 2 ‖ 2 Kings 4. 29 ‖ Ps. 2. 6 ‖ Is. 51. 16 58. 1 ‖ Jer. 23. 21, 31 | 28. 15 ‖ Ezek. 5. 1 Amos. 7. 15 ‖ S. Matt. 4. 19 | 14. 28 ‖ Acts 1. 24 8. 26 | 9. 6 *l* ‖ Rom. 1. 1 ‖ Heb. 5. 4.

373. *That* GOD *sometimes chooses preachers out of the greatest sinners.*

Gen. 28. 1   Ex. 2. 21 ‖ Ruth 4. 13 ‖ 1 Kings 25. 40 ‖ Job 21. 9 | 28. 2 | 38. 16 ‖ Ps. 18. 44 59. 12 | 68. 23 | 87. 4 | 147. 16 ‖ Prov. 27. 27 31. 14 ‖ Eccles. 12. 5   Cant. 2. 4 ‖ Is. 13. 5 17. 2 | 35. 7 | 42. 10 | 55. 13 | 60. 4 *l* | 65. 10 *l* Jer. 3. 1 | 8. 19 | 30. 10 *m* | 31. 8 | 51. 48 ‖ Ezek. 16. 42 ‖ Hos. 2. 14   Zech. 12. 7   S. Matt. 20. 12 5. 18 | 8. 3 ‖ S. Luke 15. 20 ‖ Acts 2. 8 | 13. 46 Rom. 5. 20.

374. *That* GOD, *of His grace, gives preaching and preachers.*

Deut. 11. 13, 14   Job 31. 26 ‖ Is. 13. 17 | 32. 3 41, 17 ‖ Jer. 16. 16 | 48. 12 ‖ Ezek. 33. 22 *l* Amos 2. 11.

375. *That* GOD, *out of his anger, takes away preaching and preachers.*

Deut. 11. 16   1 Sam. 13. 19 ‖ 2 Sam. 1. 21 1 Kings 17. 7 ‖ Job 9. 5 | 18. 12 | 36. 27 ‖ Ps. 119. 11 Prov. 12. 23 | 23. 9   Is. 3. 1 | 5. 6 *l* ‖ Jer. 3. 3 5. 24 | 9. 10 *f* | 12. 4 | 14. 2, 17 ‖ Lam. 1. 11 Ezek. 3. 26 ‖ Hos. 2. 9 ‖ Amos. 4. 5 | 5. 15 | 8. 11 Hag. 1. 9 ‖ S. Matt. 7. 6.

(110)

376. *That good life as well as good doctrine is necessary to preachers.*

Gen. 24. 10 | 46. 34 | 49. 20 ‖ Ex. 12. 11 | 30. 18
33. 13 Lev. 1. 14 | 7. 31 ‖ 1 Sam. 5. 2 Ezra 7. 10
Job 29. 20 | 39. 19 Ps. 50. 16 | 73. 27 | 88. 12
104. 8 Prov. 25. 4 Cant. 5. 5 | 8. 10 Is. 11. 8
30. 22 | 33. 16 | 40. 9 | 41. 15 | 42. 11 ‖ Jer. 31. 6
Hos. 10. 1 Mic. 4. 13 | 5. 9 Hag. 2. 18 ‖ Wis. 1. 4
9. 15 Ecclus. 18. 19, 20 ‖ S. Matt. 5. 13, 19 *l*
S. John 8. 7 | Acts 1. 1 *l* | 20. 28 *f* | Rom. 2. 13
1 Cor. 4. 20 | 2. 27 | 13. 1 S. James 1. 22 ‖ Rev. 11. 4.

377. *Of the unity or concord of preachers.*

Gen. 45. 24 ‖ Num. 11. 29   1 Sam. 6. 12
Job 31. 38 | 38. 37 ‖ Ps. 72. 3 | Cant. 4. 9 *l*
Judith 15. 4.

378. *That preaching is fruitful or unfruitful, according as to the preacher is faithful or unfaithful.*

Gen. 8. 11 ‖ Job 5. 19, 24 | 6. 6 | 12. 15, 20
29. 11, 21 ‖ Prov. 13. 22 | 25. 4 ‖ Is. 1. 30 | 54. 14
55. 10   Ezek. 34. 18   Hos. 9. 14, 16 | S. Luke
24. 32 ‖ Acts 10. 44 ‖ Rev. 3. 8.

379. *That preaching ought to be according to time and place and the capacity of the hearers; and that if it be infrequent, it is not sufficient, and that if it be too frequent, it is despised.*

Gen. 44. 1 Job 26. 8 | 30. 2 | 38. 36 ‖ Ps. 1. 3
25. 11   Eccles. 3. 7 ‖ Ecclus. 20. 7, 22 | 32. 7
S. Luke 5. 3 | 12. 42 ‖ S. John 16. 12 | 1 Cor. 2. 6.

380. *That sometimes we must preach when our hearers are unwilling to listen.*

Is. 62. 1 ‖ Jer. 2. 2 | 7. 2 | 11. 6 | 17. 19 | 26. 2.

381. *That God's mysteries are not to be revealed or preached to the wicked.*

Gen. 29. 27 | 44. 1 | Ex. 21. 33 || 2 Kings 20. 13 Ps. 119. 11 Prov. 9. 7 Is. 39. 2 Dan. 12. 4, 9 Mic. 1. 10 || S. Matt. 7. 6 | 11. 25 | 13. 33 Rev. 5. 11.

382. *That the labourer is worthy of his hire; or, that they who labour in spiritual things deserve a temporal reward.*

Gen. 3. 19 | 24. 33 Num. 31. 27 || Deut. 25. 4 Ps. 81. 2 | 128. 2 | 147. 8 Prov. 22. 7 || S. Matt. 10. 9 || S. Mark 6. 8 S. Luke 10. 4 1 Cor. 9. 7 Gal. 6. 8 || 2 Thess. 3. 8, 10, 12 | 2 Tim. 2. 6.

383. *Against those that live to themselves alone, and will not preach; or against those who hide the Lord's talent.*

Gen. 4. 9 | 24. 28 | 29. 10 7 | 41. 56 | 43. 3 Job 4. 2 Prov. 5. 16 | 11. 26 | 14. 33 | 22. 9 31. 24 || Ecclus. 11. 1 Is. 2. 3 | 6. 5 | 11. 4 7 21. 14 | 32. 20 51. 1 56. 10 | 58. 1 | 60. 11 Jer. 31. 10 | 50. 14 | 51. 6 Hos. 2. 21 6. 1 | 8. 9 Joel. 2. 1 || Amos 2. 2 || Ecclus. 4. 25 || 20. 30 24. 31 || S. Matt. 2. 11 | 5. 14 | 10. 27 | 25. 24 27. 52 || S. Mark 5. 30 || S. Luke 1. 39 | 19. 20 S. John 1. 41 | 4. 28 | 18. 20 || 21. 19 || S. James 5. 20 || S. Jude 12.

384. *Of the effect of preaching.*

Num. 10. 35 || Deut. 32. 42 || 2 Sam. 22. 31 Job 28. 3 | 37. 2 | 38. 34 Ps. 18. 8, 14, 30 | 32. 6 77. 17 | 93. 4 | 104. 11 | 107. 20 | 147. 18 || Prov. 30. 5 || Eccles. 12. 11 Cant. 5. 6 *m* || Is. 17. 7 50. 2 | 51. 16 || Jer. 5. 14 | 10. 13 | 23. 29 | 51. 16 Ezek. 1. 25 | 3. 22 | 37. 4 || Hos. 4. 6 | 11. 10 Nah. 1. 4 || Hab. 2. 9 7 || Zech. 10. 8 || S. Matt. 17. 17 || S. Luke 24. 32 S. John 5. 25 || Acts 2. 3 Heb. 4. 12 || Rev. 1. 16 || 4. 5.

385. *Of hunger for the Word of* God.

1 Sam. 13. 19 ‖ 1 Kings 17. 7 ‖ 2 Kings 4. 38 *f*
6. 25 *f* ‖ Ps. 105. 16 ‖ Prov. 29. 18 ‖ Is. 3. 1 | 6. 6
15. 6 | 33. 18 ‖ Jer. 6. 29 ‖ Lam. 4. 4 ‖ Hos. 4. 1
Joel 1. 9, 20 ‖ Amos 8. 11 ‖ S. Mark 8. 2 ‖ S. Luke
16. 20 ‖ S. James 5. 17.

386. *That the Word of* God *must be obeyed, and not heard only.*

Gen. 32. 24 ‖ Ex. 28. 33 ‖ Ps. 111. 10 | 119. 1
128. 1 ‖ Prov. 7. 3 ‖ Cant. 2. 14 *m* ‖ Is. 20. 2
Lam. 3. 41 ‖ Ezek. 3. 3, 27 *m* ‖ S. Matt. 5. 19 *l*
13. 23 ‖ S. Mark 4. 20 ‖ S. Luke 8. 15 | 11. 28
S. John 1. 39 ‖ Acts 1. 1 *l* ‖ Rom. 2. 13 ‖ 1 Cor.
4. 20 ‖ 2 Tim. 4. 5 ‖ S. James 22. 1 ‖ Rev. 10. 9.

387. *Of those who believe for a time.*

Ecclus. 19. 12 | 21. 18 | 22. 7 ‖ S. Matt. 7. 26
S. Mark 4. 16 ‖ S. Luke 8. 6.

Third Part.

388. *Of the duty of masters to their servants.*

Job 31. 13 ‖ Judith 16. 23 *m* ‖ Ecclus. 7. 21
33. 31 ‖ Col. 4. 1 ‖ Eph. 6. 9.

389. *Of the duty of servants towards their masters.*

Gen. 16. 9 ‖ S. Matt. 25. 20 ‖ S. Luke 19. 17
Rom. 13. 1 ‖ Eph. 6. 5 ‖ 1 S. Pet. 2. 18.

390. *Of faithfulness.*

Prov. 20. 6 *l* | 25. 13, 19 | 28. 20 *f* | Ecclus.
6. 14, 15 | 20. 23 | 29. 3 ‖ S. Matt. 24. 45 ‖ S. Luke
12. 42 ‖ S. John 1. 47 ‖ 2 Cor. 1. 17.

Fourth Part.

391. *That the righteous are ridiculed and suffer persecution in the present life.*

Gen. 4. 8 | 15. 13 | 16. 4 | 19. 9 | 21. 9 | 26. 14 27. 41 | 31. 23 | 37. 4   Ex. 1. 12 ‖ Num. 16. 3 1 Sam. 21. 14 | 23. 14   2 Sam. 16. 7 | 2 Chron. 30. 10 ‖ Job 2. 9 | 12. 4 | 19. 18 | 30. 1, 9 | Ps. 2. 2 3. 2 | 22. 12 | 69. 11 | 83. 2 | 109. 4   Prov. 14. 2 19. 28 | 29. 10, 27 | Is. 36. 4 | 53. 2 ‖ Jer. 17. 15 20. 8 ‖ Lam. 2. 16 | 3. 14 ‖ Wis. 5. 3   S. Matt. 27. 29 ‖ S. Luke 23. 11 ‖ S. John 8. 48 | 15. 19 Acts 26. 14 ‖ 1 Cor. 4. 9 ‖ S. James 2. 6.

392. *That God is no accepter of persons.*

Deut. 10. 17 | 16. 19 ‖ 2 Chron. 19. 7 ‖ Is. 42. 2 Acts 10. 34 ‖ Rom. 2. 11 ‖ Eph. 6. 9 *l* ‖ Col. 3. 25 *l* S. James 2. 2.

393. *Against those who oppress the poor and the miserable; and against rapine and calumny.*

Gen. 14. 16 ‖ Ex. 20. 15 | 22. 1, 21 ‖ Deut. 27. 17 1 Sam. 24. 14 | 30. 8, 16 ‖ 2 Kings 5. 2 | 6. 23 Job 1. 17 | 4. 10, 11 | 20. 18 | 24. 2 | 29. 12 Ps. 17. 12 | 26. 12 | 53. 5 | 58. 6 | 82. 3 | 94. 6 104. 21 | 109. 15 | Prov. 1. 11 | 10. 25 | 11. 24 21. 7 | 22. 16, 22, 28 | 23. 10, 11 | 28. 15, 24 | 30. 14 Eccles. 4. 1 | 5. 8 ‖ Is. 1. 17 ‖ 3. 11 | 3. 14 *l* | 10. 1 14. 2 | 30. 12 | 33. 1 | 54. 14 *m* | 61. 8 ‖ Jer. 2. 3, 34 5. 26 | 17. 11 | 21. 12 | 22. 3, 13 ‖ Ezek. 19. 2 32. 27 | Amos 3. 9 | 4. 1 ‖ Mic. 2. 1 | 3. 2 | 5. 1 Nah. 2. 12 | 3. 1 | Hab. 1. 3, 13 | 2. 12 | 13. 14 *l* Zech. 8. 16 *l* ‖ Mal. 3. 5 ‖ Ecclus. 4. 9, 30 | 13. 19 34. 20 ‖ 1 Macc. 9. 36, 40 ‖ S. James 2. 6.

394. *Against those who harshly rebuke the poor.*

   Prov. 14. 31 ‖ Ecclus. 4. 2 | 18. 15 ‖ S. Luke 16. 21.

395. *That the evil are not permitted to put forth all their malice against the good.*

   Gen. 19. 10 | 31. 24 ‖ Job 2. 6 | 41. 20 ‖ Ps. 33. 7 104. 9 ‖ Prov. 10. 25 ‖ Is. 50. 2 *l.*

396. *That the righteous are outwardly despised, but inwardly beautiful and precious.*

   Ex. 26. 7 ‖ Ps. 45. 14 ‖ Cant. 1. 5 ‖ Is. 50. 3 S. Matt. 13. 44 *f* ‖ 2 Cor. 4. 7 ‖ Rev. 6. 12.

Fifth Part.

397. *Of the instruction of children from infancy.*

   Ex. 13. 8 ‖ Deut. 11. 19 ‖ 1 Sam. 3. 13 *l* ‖ Job 1. 5 Prov. 22. 15 ‖ Jer. 9. 20 ‖ Ezek. 18. 10 ‖ Ecclus. 7. 23 | 16. 1 | 30. 1 | 41. 9 ‖ Eph. 6. 4.

398. *Of the duty of children to their parents.*

   Gen. 9. 23 | 27. 3 | Ex. 20. 12 ‖ Deut. 5. 15 27. 26 ‖ 2 Sam. 18. 9 ‖ Prov. 10. 1 | 30. 11, 17 Tobit 5. 1 | 14. 13 ‖ Ecclus. 3. 2 ‖ S. Matt. 19. 19 S. Mark 10. 19 *l* ‖ S. Luke 18. 20 *l* ‖ Eph. 6. 1 Col. 3. 20.

(115)

Sixth Part.

399. *Of the unity and eternity and power of* God.

Gen. 1. 1 ‖ Ex. 3. 14 ‖ Deut. 6. 4 | 32. 39
Job 9. 19 | 12. 9 | 14. 4 | 23. 13 | 25. 8 | 36. 22
38. 4 Is. 40. 28 | 43. 11, 25 | 44. 6. 24 | 45. 18, 21
46. 9 | 48. 12 | 57. 15 ‖ Dan. 4. 34 Mal. 3. 6
Ecclus. 1. 8 | 18. 1 | 24. 5 | 43. 31 ‖ Rom. 11. 33
Rev. 1. 8 | 22. 13.

400. *Of the Trinity; and plurality of Persons.*

Gen. 1. 26 | 18. 2 Job 26. 13 | 32. 8 | 33. 4
38. 6 ‖ Ps. 2. 7 | 33. 9 | 110. 1 Prov. 8. 30 | 30. 4 *l*
Is. 6. 3 | 48. 16 ‖ Dan. 7. 9 ‖ Wis. 1. 7 | 2. 16
7. 25 | 12. 1 Ecclus. 1. 5 | 51. 10 ‖ S. Matt. 3. 16
10. 20 | 12. 50 | 28. 19 S. Mark 1. 10 ‖ S. Luke
3. 22 | 22. 42 | 23. 34 ‖ S. John 3. 34 | 8. 16, 54
10. 30 | 14. 6 ‖ Rev. 4. 8 | 5. 13.

401. *Of the Eternal* Word *and His eternal generation.*

Ps. 2. 7 | 19. 2 *‖* 33. 6 | 45. 1 | 119. 89 | 147. 18
Is. 40. 8 | 53. 8 | 55. 10. 11 Wis. 9. 1 | 18. 15
S. John 1. 1 | 14. 2, 10 | 16. 28 | 17. 8, 25 ‖ 1 S.
John 1. 1 | 5. 7 Rev. 1. 2 | 19. 13 *l*.

402. *Of the Incarnation and Nativity of* Christ.

Gen. 24. 2 | 49. 10 Ex. 4. 13 | 31. 2 Num. 17. 2
24. 17 Deut. 8. 15 ‖ Judg. 6. 37 | 13. 2 ‖ 1 Kings
8. 12 ‖ Job 31. 35 | 33. 23 | 38. 6 Ps. 2. 7 | 72. 6
77. 14 | 80. 1 | 110. 1 | 144. 5 | Prov. 30. 4 | 31. 10
Eccles. 7. 28 ‖ Cant. 3. 11 Is. 1. 9 | 2. 2 | 4. 1
7. 14 | 8. 1 | 9. 6 | 11. 1 | 16. 1 | 19. 1 | 28. 16
35. 4 | 40. 9 | 42. 1 | 46. 11 | 49. 1 | 52. 13 | 53. 8
54. 1 | 55. 4 | 60. 1 | 61. 1 | 62. 1 | 64. 1 | 65. 1 *l*
66. 7 Jer. 14. 8 | 15. 10 ‖ 23. 5 | 31. 22 ‖ Ezek.
34. 23, 29 ‖ Dan. 2. 44 | 3. 25 | 7. 13 | 9. 24
Hos. 1. 11 | 2. 19 | 6. 1 | 11. 1 | 13. 14 | 14. 5
Joel 2. 23 Amos 4. 12 ‖ Jon. 1. 2 ‖ Mic. 1. 3. 15

5. 2 ‖ Hab. 2. 2 ‖ Hag. 2. 6 ‖ Zech. 2. 10 | 3. 3, 8
8. 23 | 9. 9 | 13. 1 ‖ Mal. 3, 1 | 4. 2 | Wis. 18. 14
Ecclus. 38. 4 ‖ Bar. 3. 37 ‖ 1 Macc. 14. 41 ‖ S.
Matt. 3. 17 ‖ S. Luke 1. 30.

403. *Of the manifold appearances of the* LORD.

Gen. 18. 2 | 32. 24 ‖ Ex. 3. 2 | 13. 21 | 19. 9, 18
24. 17 | 33. 9 ‖ Num. 22. 9 | 23. 4 | 24. 16 ‖ Deut.
5. 22 ‖ Judg. 13. 18 ‖ Ps. 29. 5 | 99. 7 ‖ S. Matt.
10. 20 | 17. 5 | 21. 28 ‖ S. Mark 6. 48 | 9. 7
S. Luke 9. 35 | 24. 31 ‖ S. John 2. 14 | 21. 4
Rom. 1. 16 ‖ 2 Cor. 13. 3 ‖ Heb. 1. 1 ‖ 1. S. Pet.
2. 21 ‖ Rev. 1. 13.

404. *Of the Passion of the* LORD, *and its bitterness.*

Gen. 4. 8 | 9. 20 | 22. 2, 9 | 37, 18. 23 | 49. 9
Ex. 12. 3 ‖ Lev. 1. 2 | 2. 4 | 3. 7 | 4. 5, 13, 22
Num. 13. 23 | 19. 3 ‖ Deut. 16. 5, 6 ‖ Josh. 8. 26
Judg. 16. 3, 16, 29 ‖ 1 Sam. 19. 1, 13 | 21. 13
1 Kings 21. 9 | 22. 24 ‖ 2 Chron. 24. 20 | 29. 24
Job 16. 9, 11 | 30. 1 ‖ Ps. 22. 17, 18 | 35. 16, 21
41. 9, 10 | 55. 13 | 69. 4, 8, 9, 21, 22 | 88. 3, 7, 18
109. 15 *l* | 110. 7 | 142. 4 ‖ Cant. 1. 3 | 3. 11 | 7. 7
8. 5 ‖ Is. 10. 33 | 11. 10 | 50. 6 ‖ 53. 2 | 63. 1
Jer. 11. 19 ‖ Lam. 1. 15 *l* | 3. 1 | 4. 20 ‖ Dan.
9. 24, 26 ‖ Jon. 1. 17 | 2. 6 ‖ Mic. 5. 1 *l* | Hab. 3. 4 *m*
Zech. 3. 2 | 9. 11 | 11. 12 | 13. 6 ‖ Wis. 2. 12
S. Matt. 21. 39 | 26. 14, 56 *l*, 70 | 27. 3, 26, 28
S. Luke 20. 14 ‖ S. John 19. 16.

405. *How we ought to imitate the* LORD's *Passion, and
fulfil it in ourselves.*

Prov. 31. 13 *l* ‖ S. Luke 22. 15 ‖ S. John 15. 9
17. 18 | 20. 21 *l*, 37 | Rom. 5. 3 | 1 Cor. 15. 31
Gal. 6. 14 ‖ Ephes. 5. 1 ‖ Philip. 2. 5 ‖ Col. 1. 24
Heb. 13. 13 ‖ 1 S. Pet. 2. 21 *m* | 4. 1.

406. *Of following* CHRIST.

Ex. 3. 2 | 13. 21 || Ruth 1. 16 | Cant. 1. 3 | 8. 6
Ezek. 1. 20 || S. Luke 5. 11 | 9. 57 || S. John 13. 13
Acts 12. 8 *l* || Philip. 2. 5 | 3. 17.

407. *Of the effect of the* LORD'S *Passion, and that by its application to ourselves, all our sins are blotted out.*

Gen. 37. 24 || Judg. 16. 1 || 2 Sam. 23. 20
Is. 42. 8 | Jer. 38. 6 || Dan. 6. 16 *f* || Hos. 13. 14
Zech. 9. 11 || Rom. 5. 17 | Eph. 5. 25 || Philip. 2. 6
Col. 2. 14 || 1 S. Pet. 2. 24 | 3. 18.

408. *That the memory of the* LORD'S *Passion gives comfort and sweetens all evils.*

Ex. 12. 13 | 15. 25 | 28. 38 || Num. 20. 11 | 21. 8
Josh. 2. 21 || 1 Sam. 2. 16 | 1 Kings 17. 3 || 2 Kings
4. 40 || Ps. 25. 20 | 104. 18 || Prov. 3. 18 | 31. 26
Eccles. 9. 14 | Cant. 1. 13 | 2. 3, 14 | 8. 6 || Is. 2. 10
Ezek. 9. 6 | Ecclus. 14. 25 | 29. 17 || 38. 4 || 1 Macc.
6. 34 || Heb. 12. 3.

409. *Of the mysteries of the Cross, and its virtues and types.*

Ex. 14. 16 | 15. 25 | 33. 20 || Num. 10. 36 | 13. 24
20. 8 | 21. 8 | Ezek. 9. 4 || Joel 2. 2 *m* || Wis. 10. 4 *l*
Ecclus. 38. 5 || S. John 3. 14 || Rev. 7. 3.

410. *Of the Resurrection of the* LORD.

Gen. 49. 9 || Deut. 33. 7 || Judg. 16. 3 || Ps. 3. 5
4. 3 | 7. 6, 8 | 9. 10 | 17. 6, 13 | 20. 5 | 22. 19
30. 3, 9 | 41. 8 *l*, 10 *l* | 57. 9 *l* | 78. 66 | 86. 13
139. 1, 18 | 142. 9 || Hos. 6. 2 | 13. 14 | Jon. 1. 17 *l*
2. 10 || S. Matt. 12. 49 | 16. 21 | 20. 18, 19 | S. Mark
16. 6 || S. Luke 11. 30 || Acts 10. 40 || Rom. 6. 9
1. Cor. 15. 3, 20 || Gal. 1. 1.

(118)

411. *Of the Ascension of the* LORD.

Gen. 5. 24 | 28. 12 || Ex. 14. 15 | 24. 2 || Deut. 33. 26 || Judg. 16. 3 || 2 Kings 2. 11 || Ps. 8. 1 *l* 18. 10 | 19. 6 | 21. 13 | 24. 7 | 47. 5 | 55. 6 | 68. 8 Prov. 30. 4 *f* || Eccles. 1. 5 || Cant. 3. 9 | 7. 8 Is. 63. 1 || Amos 9. 6 || Mal. 3. 2 || Ecclus. 44. 16 Bar. 3. 29 || S. Mark 16. 19 || S. Luke 24. 50 S. John 20. 17 *l* || Acts 1. 9.

412. *Of the coming of the* HOLY GHOST.

Gen. 1. 2 *l* || Lev. 9. 23 | Num. 11. 25 | Job 26. 13 Ps. 19. 6 | 33. 6 | 68. 18 || 104. 30 || Cant. 1. 3 | 4. 16 Is. 44. 3 || Lam. 1. 13 *f* || Ezek. 11. 19 | 36. 26 37. 9 || Joel 2. 28 || Wis. 1. 7 || S. Luke 24. 49 S. John 14. 16, 26 | 16. 7. 13 | 20. 22 || Acts 1. 4, 8 2. 1 | 10. 44 || Rom. 5. 5 || 2 Cor. 1. 21 | 5. 5.

413. *Of the anger and vengeance of* GOD.

Ps. 2. 5 | 6. 1 | 78. 31 | 95. 11 | 103. 9 || Prov. 6. 34 || Ezek. 7. 19 || Nah. 1. 6 || Zeph. 1. 18 3. 8 || Zech. 10. 3 || Wis. 5. 20.

414. *Of the severity and equity of Divine justice.*

Gen. 3. 14 | 4. 11, 24 | 6. 5 | 7. 21 | 19. 24 Ex. 8. 2 || 12. 29 | 14. 28 | 15. 3 | 21. 24 | 32. 33 34. 7 || Lev. 10. 2 || Num. 11. 33 | 12. 9 | 14. 12, 28 15. 35 | 16. 31, 49 | 20. 12 | 21. 6 | 25. 4, 7 || 31. 2 Deut. 5. 9 | 17. 2 | 18. 19 | 19. 18 | 21. 18 | 22. 20 25. 2 | 27. 15 | 28. 15 | 32. 19, 41 || Josh. 7. 12 24. 19 || Judg. 1. 7 | 2. 20 | 9. 23, 53 | 20. 21, 25, 46 1 Sam. 2. 31 | 4. 10, 18 | 8. 11 | 13. 13 | 15. 23, 33 17. 51 | 31. 4 || 2 Sam. 15, 16 || 16. 11 | 17. 23 18. 9 | 21. 15 | 24. 15 || 1 Kings 9. 9 *l* | 13. 2, 21 16. 2 | 18. 40 | 20. 36, 42 | 21. 19 | 22. 38 || 2 Kings 1. 3 | 2. 23 | 5. 26 | 7. 17 | 9. 36 *m* | 15. 5 | 17. 18 19. 35 || 20. 17 | 21. 12 *m* || 1 Chron. 21. 14 || Esth. 7. 10 || Ps. 3. 1 | 7. 13 | 9. 5 | 10. 16 | 11. 7 | 18. 42 21. 9 | 28. 4 | 29. 5 | 31. 19, 26 | 34. 16 | 37. 15, 20, 37

49. 19 | 50. 21 *m* | 52. 6 | 53. 6 | 54. 7 | 55. 9, 24
57. 7 | 59. 12 | 60. 12 | 68. 30 | 70. 2 | 71. 11
73. 18 | 74. 23 | 75. 3, 8 || 76. 6 | 78. 31, 45, 60
79. 6, 13 | 82. 8 | 83. 13 | 92. 8 | 94. 1, 23 | 96. 13
106. 17, 26, 39 | 107. 41 | 108. 13 | 109. 6, 28
129. 4, 6 | 135. 8 | 136. 10 | 140. 10 | 145. 20
146. 9 || Prov. 1. 24 | 21. 13 | 26. 27 || Is. 2. 12
3. 18 || Ezek. 22. 31 | 30. 9 || Hos. 5. 14 | 12. 2
13. 7 || Joel 3, 4 || 1 Macc. 7. 42 || 2 Macc. 5. 7, 9
9. 28 | 13. 8 | 15. 33 || S. Matt. 12. 31 | 18. 6
21. 19, 44 | 22. 14 | 24. 27 | 25. 26, 41 || 26. 52
S. Luke 16. 25 | 18. 14 || Rev. 13. 10 | 18. 6.

415. *Of the terror of the Day of Judgment.*

Deut. 32. 22 || Job 4. 14 | 19. 29 | 20. 26 | 21. 30
26. 11, 14 || Ps. 2, 5 | 9. 16 , 17 | 21. 9 | 75. 8
76. 8 | 97. 3, 5 || Eccles. 11. 8, 9 *l* | 12. 1, 14
Is. 1. 31 | 2. 12 | 3. 18 | 5, 14, 16, 24 | 13. 6, 9 | 22. 5
24. 8, 19, 21 | 25. 5, 6 | 27. 1 | 28. 2, 17 | 29. 6
30. 27, 33 | 31. 4 | 34. 1 | 42. 13, 14 | 59. 17 | 65. 13
66. 15, 24 | Jer. 2. 26 | 23. 19 | 25. 15 || Ezek. 1. 4
Dan, 7. 9 | Joel 2. 1, 30, 31 | 3. 2, 12, 16 | Obad. 15
Nah. 1. 3 *l*, 5 || Zeph. 1. 7, 10, 15 | 2. 3 || Mal.
3. 2, 5 *f* | 4. 5 || Wis. 5. 2, 18 | 6. 5 || Ecclus. 16. 18
S. Matt. 3. 10, 12 | 24. 27 | 25. 31 || Acts. 17. 30
Rom. 2. 14 | 14. 10 *l*, 12 || 1 Cor. 4, 5 | 15. 52
1 Thess. 5. 2 || 2 Thess. 1. 6 Heb. 10. 27 || S. James
5. 1 || 2 S. Pet. 3. 7, 10, 12 || Rev. 1. 7 | 14. 19
16. 19 | 18. 16, 21 | 19. 20 | 20. 12.

416. *That in the Day of Judgment all things shall be made manifest.*

Job 12. 22 | 20. 27 | 26. 6 | 34. 22 || Ps. 50. 21 *l*
73. 16 *l* || Prov. 10. 9 | 26. 26 | Eccles. 9. 1 | 12. 14
Is. 42. 16 || Jer. 23. 20 *l* || Lam. 4. 21 *m* || Dan.
7. 10 *l* || Nah. 3. 5 || Zeph. 1. 12 || Ecclus. 11. 27 *l*
16. 16 | 20. 2 *l* | 39. 27 | S. Matt. 10. 26 || 1 Cor. 4. 5
2 Cor. 5. 10 || Rev. 20. 12.

417. *That we have to stand before the judgment seat of* GOD.

Ps. 18. 24 | 60. 4 | 112. 6 | 119. 118, 120 ‖ Prov. 28. 5 | Eccles. 11. 8 | 12. 1 " Is. 41. 21   Jer. 15. 17   Hab. 2. 1 ‖ S. Matt. 24. 42 | 25. 13 ‖ S. Luke 21. 36.

418. *Of the general Resurrection.*

Gen. 8. 21 " Job 14. 11, 14 | 19. 25 ‖ Ps. 1. 5   Prov. 31. 21 | Eccles. 12, 4 " Cant. 1. 4 | Is. 26. 19   66. 22 | Ezek. 37. 1 ' Dan. 12. 2 | Joel 3. 2, 12   Zeph, 3. 8   2 Macc. 7. 9, 23 | 12. 43, 44 | 14. 46   S. Matt. 25. 31   S. Luke 20. 37 ‖ S. John 5. 28   6. 39 | 11. 24 | 12. 32 " Acts 17. 32 | 23. 6 | 26. 8   1. Cor. 15. 51   Eph. 1. 18 | 4. 13 | Philip. 3. 11, 20, 21   1 Thess. 4. 13   Heb. 11. 19, 35 ‖ Rev. 11. 11.

419. *Of the fewness of those that shall be saved.*

Gen. 22. 17   Num. 14. 16 " Cant. 7. 2 ‖ Amos 3. 2 ‖ Mic. 7. 1 " S. Matt. 22. 14 | S. Luke 17. 17   18. 8.

SEVENTH PART.

420. *Of Antichrist.*

Gen. 49. 17   Job 21. 13 | 40. 17 ‖ Ps. 9. 19   80. 13   Prov. 30. 29 " Dan. 7. 6, 23 | 8. 9, 23, 25   11. 36 | 12. 7, 11   S. Matt. 24. 15   S. Mark 12. 14   2 Thess. 2. 3, 8   1 S. John 2. 18 ‖ Rev. 10. 7   11. 7 | 16. 13 | 17. 8 | 19. 19 | 20. 9.

421. *Of the great tribulation that shall be in the time of Antichrist.*

Job 29. 2 | 49. 17   Dan. 7. 7, 23, 25 | 8. 10, 24   11. 31, 44 | 12. 10 ‖ S. Matt. 24. 19 " Rev. 11. 2   13. 7, 16.

422. *Of the coming of Enoch and Elijah against Antichrist.*

Mal 4. 5 ‖ S. Matt. 17. 11 ‖ Rev. 11. 3.

423. *Of the miserable death and damnation of Antichrist.*
   Is. 11. 4 | 25. 7 || Dan. 7. 11 | 8. 25 *l* | 11. 20
   2 Thess. 2. 8 | Rev. 19. 20.

424. *To Priests assembled in a synod.*
   Gen. 31. 38 || Deut. 4. 9 || 2 Sam. 23. 8 || 1 Kings
   20. 39, 40   Job 31. 38   Ps. 77. 20   Prov. 27. 23
   Jer. 3. 15 | 10. 21 | 17. 21   Ezek. 34. 2, 5, 10, 20, 23
   S. John 21. 17 || Acts 20. 28 || 1 S. Pet. 5. 2.

425. *To those that are to be ordained.*
   Lev. 21. 7, 17 || Num. 8. 6   1 Sam. 16. 13
   1 Kings 1. 39.   Jer. 7. 29   Ecclus. 11. 1 | 1 Macc.
   4. 41 || S. John 10. 1.

426. *To masters and scholars.*
   Josh. 1. 8 || Job. 4. 3 || Eccles. 1. 17 || Is. 8. 16
   21. 5 || Dan. 1. 17 | 12. 3 || Ecclus. 1. 26 | 6. 34
   S. Matt. 11. 29 | 12. 1   Rev. 1. 3.

427. *To poor people in hospitals.*
   Job 5. 17 || 1 Sam. 22. 2 || Ps. 41. 1 | 118. 18
   Is. 54. 7 | 66. 2 || Ecclus. 18. 21 | 38. 9 || 2 Cor.
   12. 9, 10.

428. *To buyers and sellers.*
   Prov. 20. 14 || Is. 7. 18 || Jer. 17. 11 || Ezek. 27
   Hos. 11. 12 | 12. 1, 7 || Mic. 6. 11 || 1 Macc. 3. 41
   Rev. 18. 11.

Eighth Part.

For the Festivals of Saints.

429. S. *Andrew.* Nov. 30.
   Gen. 8. 20 | 32. 10 || Num. 12. 3 || Judg. 7. 3
   2 Kings 4. 32 || Job 23. 11 | 39. 20 || Cant. 7. 8
   Is. 52. 13 || Judith 6. 13   Ecclus. 24. 14 | 45. 4
   2 Macc. 6. 19 || S. Matt. 4. 18   S. Luke 19. 4
   S. John 1. 41 || Rom. 10. 10 || Heb. 12. 2.

430. *S. Nicolas.* Dec. 6.

Ex. 31. 2 || Deut. 28. 36 | 1 Sam. 9. 15 | 1 *Sam.* 10. 24 | 1 Sam. 13. 14 | Job 29. 6 | 31. 18 || Ps. 4. 4 Prov. 8. 17, 34 || Is. 18. 5 | 28. 9 || Lam. 3. 27 Ecclus. 39. 6 | 48. 4.

431. *S. Thomas.* Dec. 21.

1 Kings 7. 13 || 2 Chron. 2. 13 || Job 42. 5 *Ps.* 42. 7 Prov. 14. 36 | Is. 44. 13 | Jer. 1. 10 | 22. 14 Zech. 4. 9 || Ecclus. 34. 23 || 1 Macc. 12. 38 || S. Matt. 7. 24 || S. John 20. 24 | 1 Cor. 3. 10.

432. *S. Agnes.* January 21.

Gen. 34. 1 | 2 Sam. 13. 1 | Prov. 31. 25 || Cant. 1. 10 | Is. 43. 2 *l* | Jer. 2. 2 || Ezek. 16. 10 Tob. 3. 14 || Judith 10. 4, 23 | 12. 14 | 15. 10 Wis. 8. 2. | Ecclus. 9. 10 | 26. 1 | 50. 9 || S. Matt. 25. 1 | 51. 1.

433. *S. Vincent.* January 22.

Gen 49. 21 | Deut. 3 11 *m* || Job 23. 10 | 33. 21 Ps. 41. 3 || Is 40. 20 || Jer. 1. 18 || *Ezek.* 3. 9 || *Wis.* 10. 12 || *Ecclus.* 38. 28 *f* | Ecclus. 41. 12 | 48. 13. *Song.* 26 | 2 Macc. 6. 19, 30 || S. John 12. 24 2 Tim. 2. 5 || Rev. 2. 7, 11, 17, 26 | 3. 12.

434. *The Conversion of S. Paul.* January 25.

Gen. 49. 27 | Num. 24. 4 | Deut. 33. 20 | 1 Sam. 10. 6 || Job 23. 16 | 28. 2 | 37. 21 | 38. 22 | 39. 9 Ps. 68. 22, 27 *f* | 114. 3 *l* | Prov. 25. 4 || Cant. 2. 17 Is. 21. 3 | 22. 20 | 37. 29 | 43. 1 | *Is.* 58. 9 || *Jer.* 18. 4 | Jer. 31. 19 || Lam. 1. 13 *m* || Hos. 11. 1 14. 1 || Zech. 6. 1 || Wis. 7. 7 || Ecclus. 8. 1 43. 22 || S. Matt. 19. 27 || Acts 9. 1.

435. *The Purification.* February 2.

1 Sam. 1. 24 || *Job* 13. 14 *l* | Ps. 48. 1, 9 || Is. 8, 17 60. 1 || *Hagg.* 2. 7 || Ecclus. 35. 6 || 2 Macc. 4. 21 *l.*

436. *The Annunciation.* March 25.

Gen. 16. 11 ‖ Ex. 25. 17 | 37. 1 ‖ Num. 24. 17 Judg. 13. 3 ‖ 1 Sam. 1. 20 | 25. 41 ‖ 1 Kings 9. 3 *m* 10. 18 ‖ 2 *Kings* 2. 20 | 2 Kings 7. 9 ‖ 2 Chron. 9. 17 Ps. 19. 5 *f* | 72. 6 | 85. 9 *l* ‖ Prov. 9. 1 | 25. 25 Cant. 2. 8 ‖ Is. 19. 1 | *Is.* 48. 7 ‖ Jer. 11. 16 | 31. 22 49. 14 *f* | 50. 44 ‖ Ezek. 17. 3, 22 | 44. 2 ‖ Judith 12. 10 ‖ Ecclus. 43. 20 ‖ Song 26.

437. *S. Mark.* April 25.

Gen. 49. 9 ‖ Deut. 33. 20 ‖ Judg. 14. 8, 14 Prov. 30. 30 | Jer. 50. 44 *f* ‖ Ezek. 19. 6 ‖ Hos. 11. 10 | Wis. 16. 24 ‖ *Ecclus.* 43. 27 ‖ 1 Macc. 3. 4 S. John 15. 1, 17 ‖ Eph. 4. 7.

438. *S. Philip and S. James.* May 1.

Ex. 5. 1 ‖ Num. 10. 2 | *Josh.* 2. 1 *f* ‖ Judg. 5. 18 2 Sam. 1. 23 ‖ 1 Kings 7. 21 ‖ Hab. 3. 11 ‖ Zech. 4. 3, 11, 12, 14 ‖ S. John 14. 1 ‖ Acts 5. 17 ‖ Rev. 11. 4.

439. *The Invention of the Cross.* May 3.

Gen. 2. 9 ‖ Ex. 15. 25 ‖ 1 Kings 17. 12 *l* Job 3. 21 *l* | *Job* 28. 20 | Job 29. 19 ‖ *Ps.* 23. 4 *l* Prov. 31. 16 ‖ *Cant.* 8. 6 ‖ *Is.* 19. 19 | 40. 20 *m* Prov. 2. 4. | 3. 18 | 8. 35 | 13. 12 ‖ S. Matt. 13. 44 ‖ S. John 3. 1 ‖ Gal. 5. 10 | 6. 14 ‖ Rev. 22. 1.

440. *S. Barnabas.* June 11.

Gen. 49. 21 *l* ‖ Is. 10. 6 | 18. 2 *m* | 42. 1 *m* 46. 9 *l* | 54. 15 ‖ Jer. 49. 14 ‖ Ecclus. 49. 2 *f* S. Matt. 19. 28 | 22. 24 ‖ Acts 13. 1.

441. *Nativity of S. John Baptist.* June 24.

Gen. 17. 16 | 41. 43 ‖ Ex. 23. 20 | 33. 2, 12 Judg. 13. 3 ‖ *Job* 38. 12 | Ps. 132. 18 ‖ Is. 41. 19 *Is.* 42. 1 | 44. 3 | 49. 1 | 51. 3 ‖ Hos. 13. 8 ‖ *Joel* 2. 22 *m* ‖ Mal. 3. 1 ‖ *Ecclus.* 48. 1. | *Bar.* 5. 4 S. Luke 1. 18, 76 ‖ S. John 5. 35 ‖ *Rev.* 19. 17.

442. *S. Peter.* June 29.

Deut. 27. 5 | 28. 13 | 1 Sam. 28. 3 *l* ‖ 2 Sam. 15. 21 | 1 Kings 4. 11 | 2 Kings 18. 6 ‖ Esth. 6. 7 | Job 23. 11 | Ps. 80. 11 ‖ Cant. 7. 8 ‖ Is. 28. 16 | 53. 4 | 62. 2 *l* | Jer. 28. 16 ‖ Judith 6. 13 ‖ Ecclus. 23. 28 | 43. 22 | 48. 4 | 49. 16 | 50. 4 ‖ Bar. 5. 4 | S. Matt. 26. 36 ‖ Acts 12. 1.

443. *S. Margaret.* July 20.

Gen. 3. 15 | Deut. 33. 29 | Judg. 4. 9 | 5. 27 | Job 16. 13 | 20. 15 | Ps. 91. 13 | Is. 51. 9 | Jer. 51. 34 ‖ Lam. 3. 55 | Tobit 7. 18 ‖ Judith 9. 9 *l* | Bar. 4. 25.

444. *S. Mary Magdalene.* July 22.

Gen. 9. 13 | *Ps.* 107. 35 | Prov. 31. 10 ‖ Cant. 6. 13 | Is. 7. 18 | 35. 6 | 41. 18 | 51. 3 | 54. 6 | 55. 13 | Jer. 3. 1 | Ezek. 16. 6 | *Ezek.* 36. 33, 34 | Hos. 2. 15 | S. John. 20. 11 | Rom. 5. 20 | 6. 19.

445. *S. James.* July 25.

Gen. 29. 20 | 1 Sam. 17. 36 | Is. 44. 25 ‖ *Hab.* 1. 10 *f* ‖ 1 Macc. 14. 2 | S. Matt. 20. 20 ‖ Acts 11. 27.

446. *Lammas Day.* August 1.

Gen. 49. 24 | Judg. 16. 21 ‖ 1 Kings 22. 27 | Job. 39. 5 | Ps. 105. 8 | 116. 14 *l* | Eccles. 4. 13 | Is. 42. 6 | Jer. 27. 2 | 37. 16 *f* | Jer. 40. 4 ‖ Ezek. 4. 8 | 19. 4, 9 | Dan. 6. 23 | Wis. 10. 15.

447. *S. Lawrence.* August 10.

Lev. 2. 7 | *Lev.* 6. 9 | *Deut.* 3. 11 ‖ 2 Chron. 24. 25 | 35. 13 | *Job.* 7. 13 | 23. 10 | 28. 1 | 30. 30 | 33. 19 | Ps. 17. 3 | 41. 3 | *Ps.* 63. 6, 7 | Ps. 102. 3 | 112. 9 | *Prov.* 25. 4 | Prov. 31. 20 | Cant. 8. 7 ‖ *Is.* 1. 25 | Is. 10. 17 | 43. 2 | Lam. 2. 3 *l* ‖ Ezek. 15. 4 | *Wis.* 3. 6 | Ecclus. 2. 5 | *Ecclus.* 27. 5 | Ecclus. 29. 12 | *Ecclus.* 38. 28 | Ecclus. 50. 8 | 51. 4 | S. Luke 24. 42 | S. John 12. 24 ‖ 2 Cor. 9. 6.

448. S. *Bartholomew.* August 24.
Gen. 37. 23 | 39. 12   Lev. 1. 6 || 1 Sam. 18. 4
Job 2. 4 || Cant. 5. 3, 7 | Joel 1. 7 || Ecclus. 38. 7
Bel. 27 | 1 Macc. 10. 62 || S. Luke 10. 30
S. Luke 22. 24 || Eph. 2. 19.

449. *The Decollation of S. John Baptist.* August 29.
2 Sam. 14. 7 | 2 Kings 6. 32 | Ezek. 24. 10
Hos. 5. 4 || Amos 5. 10   Ecclus. 9. 4 | 49. 3.

450. *The Nativity of the Blessed Virgin.* September 8.
Gen. 2. 18 | 24. 15 | Gen. 32. 26 || Ex. 37. 1
Lev. 26. 11 || Num. 24. 17 *m* || 1 Kings 10. 18
1 Kings 18. 44 *f* || Job 3. 9 · Ps. 81. 3 | Ps. 87. 6
Cant. 3. 9 | 6. 10 || Is. 11. 1 || Ezek. 29. 21   Nah.
3. 17 || Esth. 10. 6 | Ecclus. 24. 12 | S. Matt. 1. 1.

451. *The Exaltation of the Cross.* September 14.
Gen. 28. 12 || Josh. 8. 18   Ps. 46. 10 *l* | Cant.
8. 5 || Is. 5. 26 | 11. 12 | 13. 2 | 18. 3 | 49.
22 || Jer. 4. 6 *f* · Ezek. 17. 24 | 31. 5, 8 | 44. 2
Wis. 14. 7 || Ecclus. 24. 13 | S. John 3. 14 || Gal. 6. 11.

452. *S. Matthew.* September 21.
Num. 24. 7 *f* || 1 Sam. 2. 8 | 19. 24 || 1 Kings
16. 2 | 18. 44 || Job 23. 11 | 28. 2 · Ps. 113. 6, 7
Is. 41. 27 *l* | 42. 1 || Amos 9. 6 || S. Matt. 9. 9, 16
Eph. 4. 7.

453. *S. Michael and all Angels.* September 29.
Gen. 16. 9 | 19. 1 | 22. 15 | 28. 12 || Ex. 14. 19
23. 20 || Num. 22. 31 || Judg. 2. 1 | 6. 12 | 13. 3
1 Kings 19. 5 | 2 Kings 19. 35 | Job. 25. 3 | 38. 7
Ps. 34. 7 | 68. 17 | 91. 11, 13 | 103. 20, 21 | 104. 4
148. 2 || Is. 6. 2 | 33. 3 | 51. 9 *l* | 63. 10   Dan.
7. 10 *m* | 12. 1 || Zech. 9. 8   Tob. 3. 17 | 5. 4
Song 37 || 2 Macc. 10. 29 || S. Matt. 18. 10 | 26. 53
28. 2 || S. Luke 1. 11, 26 | 22. 43 || S. John 5. 4
Acts 12. 11 | Rom. 8. 38 | Gal. 1. 8 | Eph. 6. 12
Col. 1. 16 | 2. 15 | 1 S. Pet. 1. 12 *l* | S. Jude 9
Rev. 1. 1 *l* | 7. 9 | Rev. 8. 3 | Rev. 12. 7 | 14. 1
14. 15.

454. *S. Luke the Evangelist.* October 18.

Deut. 25. 4 ‖ Prov. 14. 4 *l* ‖ Is. 1. 3 *f* | 11. 7 *l* Ecclus. 10. 10 *f* | Ecclus. 38. 1, 3, 4, 7 | 43. 18 50. 4 ‖ S. Luke 10. 1 ‖ Eph. 4. 7.

455. *S. Simon and S. Jude.* October 28.

Gen. 35. 2 ‖ Judg. 5. 18 ‖ 1 Kings 7. 15 ‖ Cant. 8. 6 *l* ‖ Dan. 12. 3 ‖ 1 Macc. 2. 65 ‖ S. Matt. 5. 1 Rom. 8. 28.

456. *All Saints.* November 1.

Gen. 2. 9 | 22. 17 ‖ Judg. 5. 20 ‖ Job. 9. 9 Ps. 84. 4 ‖ Prov. 16. 11 *l* ‖ Cant. 3. 9 ‖ Jer. 49. 31 Dan. 12. 10 ‖ Wis. 4. 15 ‖ Ecclus. 43. 10 Ecclus. 50. 6 ‖ 1 Macc. 6. 39 ‖ S. Matt. 5. 1 ‖ Heb. 11. 33 ‖ Rev. 7. 1.

457. *S. Martin.* November 11.

Gen. 40. 9 ‖ Ruth 3. 9 ‖ 1 Sam. 18. 4 ‖ Ezra 9. 3 ‖ Job 22. 26 ‖ Ps. 16. 9 | 25. 14 ‖ Prov. 22. 2 Is. 2. 20 ‖ Lam. 3. 29 ‖ Tobit 4. 7 ‖ Ecclus. 50. 1 S. Matt. 25. 14, 36 *f*.

458. *S. Edmund.* November 20.

Gen. 49. 23 ‖ Job 16. 14 | 30. 17 ‖ Ps. 38. 2 Lam. 3. 12, 13.

459. *S. Clement.* November 23.

Job 28. 11 ‖ Ps. 46. 4 | 66. 5 ‖ Is. 51. 10 ‖ Jer. 40. 5 *l*.

460. *S. Katharine.* November 25.

Ps. 45. 3 *m*, 14 ‖ Is. 29. 14 *l* | 44. 25 *l* ‖ Ezek. 16. 18 ‖ Judith 14. 18 *m* ‖ Wis. 8. 10 ‖ 1 Cor. 1. 19

461. *The Festivals of Apostles.*

Gen. 17. 20 *l* ‖ 42. 13, 32 | 49. 28 ‖ Ex. 15. 27 39. 14 ‖ Num. 13. 16 ‖ Josh. 4. 2 ‖ Judg. 5. 4 *l* 1 Kings 4. 7 ‖ Job 37. 11 ‖ Ps. 19. 1 | 45. 17 Is. 60. 8 ‖ Mic. 5. 7 ‖ Ecclus. 49. 10 ‖ Bar. 6. 62 Rev. 12. 1 | 24. 2.

462. *The Festivals of Evangelists.*
   Gen. 2. 10 | Ex. 25, 12, 26 || *Ps.* 19. 4 || Prov. 30. 29 || Cant. 6. 12 || Ezek. 1. 5, 17 || Zech. 1. 20 6. 1, 5.

463. *The Festival of one Martyr.*
   Gen. 4. 10 || Job 13. 14 | 16. 18 | 28. 2 | 33. 21 2 Macc. 6. 19, 30.

464. *The Festival of many Martyrs.*
   Judg. 5. 2, 20 | 7. 20 || Ps. 44. 22 || Nah. 2. 3 1 Macc. 4. 41.

465. *The Festival of one Confessor and Bishop.*
   Ex. 28. 37 || Ps. 75. 12 *l* || Prov. 20. 7 || Mal. 2. 7 Ecclus. 45. 12 | 50. 1 || 1 Tim. 3. 2 | Tit. 1. 7.

466. *The Festival of one Confessor and Doctor.*
   Gen. 24. 20 | 2. 19 | 31. 3   Ps. 81. 17 || Is. 1. 9 Joel 3. 18 *l* || Zech. 13. 1 || Mal. 4. 6 | Ecclus. 39. 9 45. 1 || S. Matt. 5. 19 *l* || S. James 5. 18.

467. *The Festival of many Confessors.*
   Judg. 5. 4 *l*, 20 || 1 Kings 12. 20 *l* || 2 Chron. 30. 12 Job 38. 31 || Ps. 89. 5   Dan. 12. 3 | Ecclus. 24. 33 39. 13 | 44, 1, 13 | 47. 9 | Bar. 3. 34.

468. *The Festival of one Virgin and Martyr.*
   Ex. 4. 25 || 2 *Kings* 2. 20 *m* || Cant. 1. 5 | 2. 13 *l* 4. 8 | Nah. 1. 4 *l* || Wis. 4. 1.

469. *The Festival of one Virgin.*
   Gen. 24. 15 || Judg. 5. 12, 25 || 2 Sam. 13. 1 1 Kings 1. 2 || Prov. 31. 39   Cant. 4. 1, 7, 12 Tobit 3. 14 || Ecclus. 26. 22 | 40. 19 *l* || Rev. 19. 7 21. 9.

470.   *The Festival of many Virgins.* ˙

   Judg. 5. 10 ‖ Esth. 2. 2, 3 ‖ Job 42. 15 ‖ Ps. 45. 15
Cant. 1. 3 *l* | 6. 1 ‖ Lam. 2. 10.

471.   *The Translation of Saints.*

   Gen. 5. 24 ‖ Ex. 16. 33 ‖ 2 Sam. 21. 13 ‖ Zech.
9. 16 *l* ‖ Wis. 4. 10 ‖ Ecclus. 44. 16 | 49. 10 *m*, 14
Heb. 11. 5.

472.   *The Dedication of a Church.*

   Gen. 28. 16 ‖ *Ex.* 3. 5 ‖ *Num.* 7. 1 ‖ *Prov.* 9. 1
Jer. 30. 18 *l*.

INDEX.

	PAGE
Accepter of persons, that God is no	113
Accuse others, against those who	62
Accusers, against	62
Active life, as regards good works	89
Adversity, against those that call upon God in, and not in prosperity	78
———— and poverty, by which the Church increases in spiritual gifts	40
———— comparison of with prosperity	77
———— we must not despair in good	77
Affections, that we must purge our's from sin, to the end that we may obtain the grace of meditation; and of holiness	93
———— that they who set their's on the things which can be seen, neglect those which cannot be seen; and the contrary	93
Afflicted and distressed, God comforts, and in His wrath remembers mercy	78
Affliction, temporal, that the Saints consider it to be a blessing, and rejoice in it	76
Afflictions of the righteous are many, but the Lord delivereth him out of all	78

	PAGE
Agnes, S.	122
Alms, to be given with cheerfulness	46
———— to whom to be given	46
———— not to be given to those who need them not	46
———— against those who offer to God of the worst they have	46
———— to be given in our lifetime	46
———— given from robbery, are not acceptable to God	46
———— offered by the wicked, will not be accepted	46
———— of the righteous, acceptable to God	46
Almsgiving, goodwill in	44
———————— pure, frequent, hearty, moderate and free	45
———————— to whom, how much, what, how, when, why from thee	45
———————— in general	45
———————— effects of	45
All Saints	126
Ambitious, the, by what signs they are distinguished	101
Andrew, S.	121
Anger and vengeance of God	118
———— and its effects	54
———— in general	54
———— must not gain dominion over the mind	54
———— that the Lord sometimes spares out of	76
Annunciation, the	123

K

	PAGE
Answers speedily, that GOD does	98
Antichrist, of	120
———— of the great tribulation that shall be in the time of	120
———— against, of the coming of Enoch and Elijah	120
———— of the miserable death and damnation of	121
Apostles, the festivals of	126
Appearances of the LORD, of the manifold	116
Armour of God	70
Ascend, that we must always	60
Ascension of the LORD, of the	118
Ask, that GOD gives more than we	98
Attention in prayer, of	99
Avarice and covetousness, and its effects	41
Backsliding, against	81
Baptism, of	71
Baptist, S. John, the Decollation of	125
Barnabas, S.	123
Bartholomew, S.	125
Beatitude, of everlasting	80
Beauty, against those that boast of their	49
Believe, of those who do for a time	112
Benefits of GOD, against the ingratitude of man for	99
———— temporal, good works not to be done for, but for the sake of GOD	53
Birth, memory of our	91
Bishop, against those who thrust themselves into the office of	101
Bitterness of the life of the wicked, concerning	82
Blasphemy, against	63
Blessing, a, is given to those who do good deeds	89

	PAGE
Boasting, against	61
———— tongue, against a	61
Body, that the outward demeanour of the, is a sign of the disposition of the soul	108
Bread of Life, of	101
Buyers and sellers, frauds of	38
———— to	121
Calamities, that we are not to lament beyond measure	58
Calumny, against riches acquired by	39
———— and rapine, against	113
Carnal desires, of	37
Charity, of	87
Chastisement of those whom GOD loves	76
Children, of the instruction of from infancy	114
———— of the duty of, to their parents	114
CHRIST, of following	117
Church, the dedication of a	128
———— increases in spiritual gifts, by poverty and adversity	40
———— that the revenues of the ought not to be given to relations, but to the poor	105
Clement, S.	126
Cogitations, of thought which weighs	86
Coming of the HOLY GHOST, of the	118
———— of Enoch and Elijah, of the, against Antichrist	120
Commandments, against those that observe the lesser and neglect the greater	53
Commands, that counsels are to be added to	60
Commendation of poverty, of	40
———— of mercy, of	44
Companionship of the wicked, that we ought to avoid	83

INDEX.

Companionship, of the usefulness of good	84
Company of the wicked, that we are sometimes to tolerate	83
Compassion, of	44
Concord and unity, and their fruits, of	57
Condescension of prelates, of the	103
Confession, and its fruit, of	72
——— contrition, and satisfaction, taken together	73
——— or conversion, against those that put off	69
——— that the burden imposed thereon is not to be out of proportion to the strength	71
——— to be prudently administered	71
——— what it ought to be	71
Confessor and Bishop, the festival of one	127
——— and Doctor, the festival of one	127
Confessors, the festival of many	127
Congratulation, of	57
Consolation, of	108
Conspiracy against others, against	56
Constancy or maturity, of	79
Contempt of riches, of the	40
Contentious, against those that are	63
Contrition, of	71
——— confession, and satisfaction, taken together	73
——— concerning the bitterness of	70
Conversation of the wicked, that we ought to avoid	83
Conversion and repentance, we ought to stir others up to	67
——— is hearty in thought and in deed, if we renounce the details of sin	68
Conversion that we are not to presume at the beginning of our	69
——— or confession, against those that put off	69
——— of S. Paul, the	122
——— of the world, and from sin, of	67
Correction, of the severe that is to be administered to the hardened	107
——— of the which brings favour and friends	106
——— should be administered with gentleness and in moderation	106
——— that a gentle may amend, where severity would harden, an offender	106
Corruption of the people which follows the ill example of a prelate, of the	103
Counsel, of	96
——— against those who despise or do not seek wholesome	96
——— against those who keep back the truth when they are called to	96
Counsels are to be added to commands	60
——— of wicked men, against the	96
——— of the wicked, that we ought to avoid	83
Covetousness, against	38
——— and avarice, and its effects	41
Crime, that punishment will answer to, both in quantity and quality	84
Cross, of the mysteries of the, and its virtues and types	117
——— the Exaltation of	125
——— the Invention of the	123
Curse, that a is given to all who do ill	90

K 2

	PAGE
Cursing, against	63
Cut short the words of the Lord, against those who	99
Daintiness, against	36
Damnation of Antichrist, of	121
Day of Judgment, of the terror of	119
——— all things shall be made manifest in the	119
Dead, that we are not to lament beyond measure the	58
Deadly sins, of the seven	65
Death, of the memory of our	91
——— of keeping in remembrance our	92
——— sudden, of others, that a good man profits from	106
——— of Antichrist, of the miserable	121
Decollation of S. John the Baptist, the	125
Dedication of a church, the	128
Deeds, that God not only sees, but also thoughts	88
Deposition and punishment of evil prelates, of the	104
Desires and longings, of	99
Despair, against	87
Detractors, against	62
Devil, that men are sold to the on account of their sins	75
——— the, assaults us more vehemently if we return to sin	81
——— of the threefold army of the	65
——— of the threefold remedy against the threefold assaults of the	65
——— against those that will not be subject to others, and thus imitate the	105
——— of the, and his fall	75
——— of the perseverance of the	74

	PAGE
Devil, that the power of the is small if a man resist	75
——— the is always desirous of rejecting heavenly, and keeping earthly things	75
——— the is cruel, and his ways are hard	75
——— the, that he endeavours to destroy one prelate more than many of those who are set under him	103
Discord, against	56
——— against those that sow	62
Discretion, of prudence which is called	85
Disobedient, against those that are	51
Distressed and afflicted, God comforts, and in His wrath remembers mercy	78
Divine justice, of the severity and equity of	118
Doctrine, holy, of	71
Dreams, against vain	58
Drinking, against excessive	36
Drunkenness, of	36
Duty of children to their parents, of the	114
Duties, of the anxiety to accomplish all	59
Ears, against sins of the	64
Eating, against excessive	36
Ecclesiastics, wicked, are worse than wicked laymen	104
——— against those that say that they ought not to be reproved before laymen	105
Edification, that all our words should be to	63
Edmund, S.	126
Egyptians, are to be spoiled, in order that the Hebrews may be enriched	96
Enemies, that we must love our	57
Enoch and Elijah, of the coming of, against Antichrist	120

INDEX.

	PAGE
Envy, in general, against	55
Equity and severity of Divine justice, of the	118
Eternal joy, ineffableness of	80
Eternity and unity, and power of God, of the	115
Evangelists, the festivals of	127
Evil, none shall go unpunished	84
—— for good, against those that return	56
—— for evil, against those that return	56
—— habit and obstinacy, of	82
—— against those that unite in doing	56
—— works, that understanding is deservedly taken away from those who do	90
—— and impenitent men die before the time which God had otherwise appointed for them	69
—— thoughts, against	91
—— against those who mix good with	81
—— fear, against an	88
—— intention, of an	53
—— solitude, against any	56
—— prelates may be rebuked by their inferiors	106
—— prelates may be reverently admonished when guilty of enormous sins	106
—— that the are not permitted to put forth all their malice against the good	114
Exaltation of the Cross, the	125
Example of a good prelate, that by it his people prospers, and is saved	103
—— of the wicked, that we ought to avoid	83
Examples, good, that we ought to follow	90
—— evil, against those who set	90
Examples of another, that one is corrected by the	106
—— evil, that we are not to imitate	90
Excel others, that a prelate or preacher ought, in his life and works, to	101
Excellency of God, of the uninvestigable	99
Expounding the Scriptures, of	108
Eyes, against sins of the	64
—— of the wicked will be opened after they are cast into hell	84
Faith, of, and its articles	86
Faithfulness, of	112
False witness and lying, of	61
Falsehood, against riches acquired by	39
Fame, of good	90
Fasting, of	37
—— indiscreet, against	37
Favour of man, that we are not to seek in our works	53
Fear, against an evil	88
Feast, of a good	37
Festivals, that we are not to indulge in idleness on	100
—— of Saints	121
Flattery, against	62
Flatterers gain favour with wicked prelates	104
Flesh, that it must be subdued to the spirit	37
Folly, against	95
Foolish men, against	95
—— mirth, against	52
Fortitude, of	85
Fragility, human, of the memory of our	91
Fraud, against riches acquired by	39
Frauds of buyers and sellers, against	38
Fewness of those that shall be saved, of the	120

	PAGE
Friends, against those that too often frequent the houses of	81
Gifts, good, to be attributed to God, and that He is to be praised for them	53
—— or graces of God, of the	65
—— of the Holy Ghost, of the seven	65
Gluttony, of	36
—— and drunkenness in common, against	36
God and mammon, none can serve	81
—— against those who forget	92
—— that we ought to keep in our memory, and in our thoughts	92
—— of the unity and eternity and power of	115
—— that we have to stand before the judgment-seat of	120
—— does not regard the supplication of sinners	98
—— is no accepter of persons	113
—— that the knowledge of, is to be sought for earnestly and indefatigably	98
—— of the love of	87
—— of the anger and vengeance of	118
—— of the grace of	44
—— for the sake of, all good works to be done, and not for the sake of temporal benefits	53
—— answers speedily	98
—— gives more than we ask	98
Good against those who return evil for	56
—— that the evil are not permitted to put forth all their malice against the	114
—— that the are despised and ridiculed of wicked prelates	104

	PAGE
Good deeds, that a blessing is given to those who do	89
—— examples, that we ought to follow	90
—— fear, against any	88
—— fame, and good savour, of	90
—— gifts are to be attributed to God, and that He is to praised for them	53
—— intention, of a	53
—— man, that a, profits from the punishment and sudden death of others	106
—— none shall go unrewarded	84
—— prelate, that by the example of a, his people prospers, and is saved	103
—— savour, and good fame, of	90
—— of the reward of the	79
—— the companionship of the, to be sought	84
—— superiors, not to be obeyed when they command that which is contrary to God's law	52
—— thoughts and meditations, of	91
—— with evil, against those that mix	81
—— works, of our being arrayed with	80
—— works, of caution and judgment in doing	89
—— works, to be done for the sake of God, and not for temporal benefits	53
—— works and prayers, wisdom to be sought by	94
—— works, that the understanding of is rightly given to those who are pure and humble	89
—— works, that we ought to hide our	54
—— works, of the active life as regards	89
—— works, of doing with gladness	59

Goodness, that we must always advance in	59
Goodwill in almsgiving, of a	44
Gospel, of preaching the	108
Grace, after the bestowal of, the devil is wont to assault us grievously	74
—— of God, of the	44
Graces or gifts of God, of the	65
Great men, against those that too often frequent the houses of	81
Greater commandments, against those that neglect the, and observe the lesser	53
Greatest men will suffer the greatest punishment	84
Habits, good, and perseverance in good, of	79
Hardened, of the severe correction that ought to be administered to the	107
Hatred, against	55
Heart, hardness of, against	43
—— instability of, against	80
—— sins of the, against	91
—— malice and depth of the	91
Hebrews, that the may be enriched, the Egyptians are to be spoiled	96
Hell, after the wicked are cast into, their eyes will be opened	84
Help of man, against those who put their hope in	40
Hide our good works, that we ought to	54
Hire, that the labourer is worthy of his	111
Holiness, that we may attain the grace of, we must purge our affections and understanding from sin	93
Holy Ghost, of the coming of the	118
Holy Ghost, of the seven gifts of the	65
Holy Scripture, of the consolation of	95
Hope, of	87
—— in the help of men, against those who put their	40
—— of the wicked, against the	40
Hospitality to the poor, of	47
Hospitals, to poor people in	121
Human fragility, of the memory of our	91
—— life, of the misery and labour of	41
—— keeping in remembrance the shortness and misery of	92
Humble and pure, that the understanding of good works is rightly given to those who are	89
Humbled, he is, that compares himself to his superiors	51
Humility, and its effects	49
—— in general	50
—— false, of the proud	51
—— that he would ascend to virtues, must first descend by	50
Hunger for the Word of God, of	112
Hypocrites, against, and by what signs they are known	53
Idleness, or listlessness, and their effects	57
—— in general, against	58
Idolators, against	81
Ill, that a curse is given to those who do	90
Ill example of a prelate, of the corruption of the people which follows	103
Impatience, against	54
Impenitent and evil men die before the time which God had otherwise appointed for them	69
Impurity, against	87

	PAGE
Incarnation, of the	115
Inconstancy, and wandering of thought, against	80
Ineffableness of eternal glory	80
Infancy, of the instruction of children from	114
Inferiors, he that compares himself to his, is made proud	51
Ingratitude of man for the benefits of God, against the	99
Instability of heart, against	80
Instructing others, of	108
Instruction of children from infancy, of the	114
Intention, good or evil	53
Invention of the Cross, of the	123
James, S.	124
John, S., Baptist, Nativity of	123
——— Decollation of	125
Joy, eternal, of the ineffableness of	80
——— spiritual, of	59
Judge rashly, against those that	63
Judgment, of the terror of the day of	119
——— day, all things shall be made manifest in the	119
——— of God, secret sin cannot long escape detection through	53
——— seat of God, that we have to stand before	120
Justice, Divine, of the severity and equity of	118
——— of	85
——— of the balance of	86
——— and mercy, union of	44
Katharine, S.	126
Knowledge, against those that boast of their	49
——— of God, to be sought for earnestly and indefatigably	98

	PAGE
Knowledge, worldly, against too much attention to	96
Labour, that we must before we can rest	89
Labourer, that he is worthy of his hire	111
Labourers, against those who keep back the pay of their	38
Lament the dead, we are not to	58
——— beyond measure calamities, that we are not to	58
Lammas Day	124
Lawful, that an oath is sometimes	62
——— that an oath is sometimes not	62
Law of God, of the continual meditation of	94
Lawrence, S.	124
Laymen, against ecclesiastics who say they ought not to be reproved before	105
Lend, against those who are unwilling to	43
Lesser commandments, against those who observe the, and neglect the greater	53
Liberality, of	45
Life, of the shortness of	52
——— against those that presume on a long	52
——— human, of the shortness and misery of	92
Listlessness or idleness, and their effects	57
Live to themselves alone, against those who, and will not preach	111
Lives of the saints are our incitements to well-doing	90
Longings and desires, of	99
Lord, the, fights for them that are His	78
——— the way of the, is narrow at the beginning, but in the end broad and pleasant	75

INDEX.

	PAGE
Lord, of the manifold appearances of the	116
—— of the Resurrection of the	117
—— of the Ascension of the	118
—— of the Passion of the	116
Lord's Passion, of the effect of the	117
—— Passion, how we ought to imitate the, and fulfil it in ourselves	116
—— Passion, that the memory of the gives comfort, and sweetens all evil	117
Loss of time, of	59
Love our enemies, that we must	57
—— of God, and one's neighbour, of	87
Loving-kindness, sweetness of God's towards the poor	43
Luke, S., the Evangelist	126
Lying and false-witness, of	61
Magdalene, S. Mary	124
Malice and depth of the heart, of	91
—— that the evil are not permitted to put forth all their against the good	114
Mammon and God, none can serve	81
Manifestation of sin, of the threefold	65
—————— of the fourfold	65
Manna, and the Bread of Life, of	101
Many, that the sin of one man is often visited on	83
Margaret, S.	124
Mark, S.	123
Martin, S.	126
Martyr, the festival of one	127
Martyrs, the festival of many	127
Mary Magdalene, S.	124
Masters, of the duty of to their servants	112
—— and scholars, to	121
Masters, of the duties of servants towards their	112
Matthew, S.	125
Maturity or constancy, of	79
Meats, daintiness in, against	36
Meditation, continual, of wisdom and of the law of God	94
—————— that we may obtain the grace of, we must purge our affections and understanding	93
—————— that in solitude we have leisure for	93
Meditations and good thoughts, of	91
Meekness, of	54
Memory of our birth, human fragility, and death	91
Men, obstinate old, against	82
—— the greatest, will suffer the greatest punishment	84
Mercy of the Lord, of the	43
—— commendation of	44
—— of man	44
—— works of	47
—— and justice, union of	44
Michael, S., and all Angels	125
Mighty men of this world, against	39
Mind, that anger must not gain dominion over the	54
Mirth, against foolish	52
Misfortunes, against those that rejoice in those of others	55
Mission of prelates or preachers, of the	109
Money, those who have acquired it unjustly are bound to restore it	39
Murder, against	56
Murmur, against those that	63
—— against the works of God, those that	63
Mysteries are not to be revealed or preached to the wicked	111
—— of the Cross, of the, and its virtues and types	117

	PAGE
Nativity of CHRIST, of the..	115
———— of S. John Baptist..	123
———— of the Blessed Virgin	125
Neglect small things, against those who	59
Negligent, against those that are	59
Neighbour, love of GOD and one's	87
New man, that we must put off the old man, and put on the	66
Newly-converted, to the ...	69
———— those that are, to be gently treated	69
Nicolas, S.	122
Oath, sometimes lawful	62
———— sometimes not lawful	62
Oblations of the righteous, acceptable to GOD	46
Obstinacy and evil habit, of..	82
Obstinate old men, against	82
Obedience, and its commendation, of	51
Occupations, of those that have too many	94
Old man, that we must put off the, and put on the new man	66
Omissions and venial sins, against	59
One is corrected by the example of another	106
———— man's sin often visited on many	83
Operation, of, which weighs that which is done, or to be done	86
Oppress the poor and the miserable, against those who..	113
Ordained, to those that are to be	121
Others' salvation, that we ought to be anxious for....	67
———— that it is advantageous to pray for	98

	PAGE
Pacify tumults, of those that	57
Parents, of the duty of children to their	114
Passion of the LORD, of the, and its bitterness	116
———— the LORD's, how we ought to imitate, and fulfil it in ourselves	116
———— of the effect of the LORD's: and that by its application to ourselves, all our sins are blotted out....	117
———— of the LORD, that the memory of gives comfort and sweetens all evils	117
Pastoral care, of	102
Patience, of	55
Paul, S., the Conversion of .	122
Pay of their labourers, against those who keep back the ..	38
Peace, that we are to keep, with all	57
Penitence, and the arms of ..	70
———— of sinners well-pleasing to GOD	72
People, that they suffer for the example of evil prelates	103
Perfect, that he who is, ought to consider himself imperfect	50
Perjury, against	61
Perseverance in good, of	79
———— of the Devil, of the	74
Persons, GOD is no accepter of..	113
Peter, S.	124
Philip and James, SS.	123
Pluralities, against	105
Poor and miserable, against those who oppress the	113
———— sweetness of GOD's lovingkindness towards the	43
———— against those who harshly rebuke the	114
———— visiting of, and hospitality to the	47
———— people in hospitals, to ..	121
Poverty, commendation of the	40

	PAGE
Poverty and adversity, by which the Church increases in spiritual gifts	40
Power of GOD, of the	115
Powerful, that the righteous ought not to fear the	88
Praise of GOD, of the	99
—— of GOD, that we are to labour in on Sundays and festivals	100
Pray for others, that it is advantageous to	98
—— that the thoughts of this world ought to be banished when we	97
—— for what we ought to	97
Prayer, and its efficacy, of	97
—— and good works, wisdom is to be sought by	94
—— of attention in	99
—— perseverance in	98
—— and preaching, that we are to labour in on Sundays and festivals	100
Prayers, if we would have them efficacious, we must first prepare our life	97
—— that we must add tears to our	98
Preach, that sometimes we must when our hearers are unwilling to listen	110
—— against those that live to themselves alone, and will not	111
Preacher, that every prelate ought to be a	102
—— or prelate, that a ought to excel others in his life and works	101
—— that a ought to have the Word of GOD in his heart	102
—— that a, should shew forth his knowledge by his words	102

	PAGE
Preachers, that good life as well as good doctrine is necessary to	110
—— or prelates ought first to learn before they teach	108
—— of the unity or concord of	110
—— that GOD sometimes chooses them out of the greatest sinners	109
—— and preaching, that GOD, of His grace, gives	109
—— and preaching, that GOD, out of His anger, takes away	109
Preaching, that it is fruitful or unfruitful, according as the preacher is faithful or unfaithful	110
—— that it ought to be according to time and place, and the capacity of the hearers	110
—— that if it be unfrequent it is not sufficient; and that if it be too frequent, it is despised	110
—— of the effect of	111
—— and prayer, that we are to labour in on Sundays and festivals	100
—— the Gospel, of	108
Prelate, by the example of a good, his people prospers, and is saved	103
—— that the devil endeavours to destroy one, more than many of those who are set under him	103
—— of the corruption of the people which follows the ill example of a	103
—— or preacher ought to excel others in his life and his works	101
—— that none, except he be called by GOD, should dare to be a	109

	PAGE
Prelate every, ought to be a preacher	102
—— or preacher ought first to learn before they teach	108
—————— ought to have the Word of GOD in his heart	102
—————————— should show forth his knowledge by his words	102
Prelates, of the affection of those over whom they are set	102
—— of the condescension of	103
—— that the people suffers for the sins of evil	103
—— or preachers, of the mission of	100
—— what are to be elected and how	101
—— against those that keep silence when they ought to speak	104
—— wicked, to what evil things are compared by the LORD	104
—— that flatterers gain favour with wicked, and the good are despised and ridiculed	104
—— of the zeal of	105
—— evil, that they may be rebuked by their inferiors	106
—— evil, may be reverently admonished when they are guilty of enormous sins	106
—— evil, of the punishment and deposition of	104
Presume, that we are not to at the beginning of our conversion	69
Presumption, of	88
Pride, against, and its effects	47
—— causes of	48
—— of, in common	49
Priest, or any one that is called to rebuke, ought to correct himself before he corrects others	106
Priests, assembled in a synod, to	121
Profane songs, against	99
Progress, of the fervour of, and the anxiety to accomplish all duties	59
Promise or vow, against indiscreetly	62
Prosperity, we must not be puffed up in evil	77
—————— comparison of, with adversity	77
—————— against those that call not upon GOD in, but do in adversity	78
—————— is the cause of pride, luxury, and forgetfulness of the mercies of GOD	78
Proud, he that compares himself to his inferiors is made	51
—— of the false humility of the	51
Prudence, of, which is called discretion	85
Punished, against those who are with the instrument of their own sin	56
Punishment and sudden death of others, that a good man profits from the	106
—————— that it will answer to crime both in quantity and quality	84
—————— that the greatest men will suffer the greatest	84
—————— and deposition of evil prelates, of the	104
Pure and humble, that the understanding of good works is rightly given to those who are	89
Purification, the	122
Pusillanimity of the wicked, of	88

INDEX. 141

Quarrelsome, against those that are 63

Rank, against those that boast of their 49
Rapine and calumny, against 113
Rashly judge, against those who 63
Rebuke, that it ought not to be administered at all times .. 107
—— against those that despise 107
—— that a priest or any one that is called to, ought to correct himself before he correct others 106
—— the poor, against those who harshly 114
Reconciliation, of 57
Rejoice in the misfortunes of others, against those who 55
Relations, against the natural desire of often visiting our 81
Repentance should be taken into hand speedily for seven reasons :—
 1. Lest sin become a habit 68
 2. Lest we should fall from one wickedness into another 68
 3. Sudden death 68
 4. Last sickness 68
 5. Lest of the torments of hell 69
 6. The difficulty of true repentance 69
 7. The shame men feel in confession of sin 69
—— and conversion, we ought to stir up others to 67
—— that even the righteous stand in need of 70
Rest, that we must labour before we can 89
Resurrection of the Lord, of the 117
—— of the general .. 120
Return to God, of those that 74

Reveal secrets, against those who 62
Revenge, against 56
Revenues of the Church are not to be given to relations, but to the poor 105
Reward of the good, of the .. 79
—— of the hope of the everlasting 79
Rich and mighty men of this world, against the 39
—— man is difficult to be saved 39
Riches, against those that boast in their 49
—— acquired by theft, fraud, calumny, and falsehood, will not endure 39
—— spiritual, of 40
—— of the contempt of 40
—— that it is lawful to possess 39
Righteous, afflictions of the, are many, but the Lord delivereth him out of all .. 78
—— are ridiculed and suffer persecution in the present life 113
—— if afflicted in this present life, how great the punishment of the wicked in the life to come 77
—— of the security of the 88
—— man, the, stands in need of repentance 70
—— ought not to fear the powerful 88
—— that they are outwardly despised, but inwardly beautiful and precious 114
—— the, may often profit by one who has fallen into sin 82
—— man, the, oblation of is acceptable to God 46
Righteousness, that our's, compared with God's, is nothing 51

	PAGE
Righteousness of the righteous, as it is well-pleasing to God, so is the penitence of sinners	72
Robber, that he is a, who does not give the revenues of the Church to the poor, rather than to relations	105
Sacraments, of the	86
Sacrilege, against	38
Saints, All	126
—— that the lives of the, are our incitements to well-doing	90
—— the Translation of	128
—— the, are fed by expectation of things eternal	79
—— that we ought to keep in memory the examples of the, that we may imitate them	92
Salvation of others, we ought to be anxious for the	67
Satisfaction, contrition, and confession, taken together	73
—— in this life, of	72
Saved, of the fewness of those that shall be	120
Scandals, of	90
Scholars and masters, to	121
Scripture, Holy, of the consolation of	95
Scriptures, of expounding the	103
Secrets, against those who reveal	62
Security of the righteous, of the	88
Seen, that they who set their affections on the things which can be seen, neglect those which cannot be	93
Sellers and buyers, against the frauds of	38
—————— to	121
Senses, of the five, and keeping them from sin	64
Servants, of the duty of masters to their	112
—— of the duty of toward their masters	112

	PAGE
Seven deadly sins, of the	65
—— gifts of the Holy Ghost, of the	65
Severity, where it would harden an offender, that a gentle correction may amend	106
—— and equity of Divine justice, of the	118
Shortness of the present life, of the	52
Signs by which hypocrites are known	53
Silence, of	64
Simon and Jude, SS.	126
Simony, against	38
Simplicity, and its commendation, of	91
Sin, of the threefold manifestation of	65
—— if we return to, the devil assaults us more vehemently	81
—— secret, cannot long escape detection, through the just judgment of God	53
—— of one man is often visited on many	83
—— of the knowledge of	92
—— and the world, of conversion from	67
—— the bodies of the wicked altogether polluted with	82
—— against those who are punished with the instrument of their own	56
—— of the fourfold manifestation of	65
—— of the first motions to	74
—— that one who has fallen back into, may often profit the righteous	82
—— as much as we have given ourselves up to, so much we ought to return to God	72
—— against, absolutely	35
—— of the weight of	35
—— of the blindness of	35
—— of the hardness of	35

	PAGE
Sin, of the chains of	35
—— of new devices in	35
—— of the ears, against	64
—— of the eyes, against	64
—— against a tongue that seduces to	63
—— of smelling, against	64
—— that there is no wisdom where it reigns	95
Sing, against those who sing undevoutly and irreverently	99
Sinners, enormous, when converted, may be profitable to others by their teaching and example	68
—— that God sometimes chooses preachers out of the greatest	109
—— that God does not regard the supplications of	98
Sins of the tongue, of the	61
—— that we ought abundantly to weep for our	70
—— of the heart, against	91
—— that we should remember our, and the benefits of God	92
—— all our, are blotted out by the application of the effect of our Lord's Passion to ourselves	117
—— against those who excuse their	107
—— against the four crying	89
—— ought frequently to recollect our, that we may better confess them	92
—— seven deadly, of the	65
—— that men are sold to the Devil on account of their	75
Small things, against those who neglect	59
Smelling, against the sin of	64
Sobriety, or temperance, of	36
Solitude, against an evil	56
—— in, that we may have leisure for the study of wisdom and for meditation	93

	PAGE
Songs, against profane	99
Sorrows of this world, against the	58
Soul, that the outward demeanour of the body is a sign of the disposition of the	108
Speech, of, which ponders that which is said, or to be said	86
Speedily, that God answers	98
Spiritual gifts, the Church increases in, by poverty and adversity	40
—— joy, of	59
—— riches, of	40
—— of the contempt of things, they who labour in deserve a temporal reward	111
Stir up others, we ought to, to repentance and conversion	67
Strength, against those that boast of their	49
—— that the burden imposed is not to be out of proportion to the	71
—— against those who ascribe their works to their own	54
Subject to others, against those who will not be	105
Sudden death of others, that a good man profits from the	106
Sundays, and other festivals, that we are not to be idle, but to labour in the praise of God, and in prayer and preaching	100
Superiors, he that compares himself to his, is humbled	51
—— good, that we are not to obey when they command that which is contrary to God's law	52
—— wicked, to be obeyed, if they command that which is consistent with God's will	52
Supplications of sinners, that God does not regard	98

	PAGE
Suspicious, against those that are	63
Swearing indiscreetly, against	61
Sweetness of GOD's loving-kindness to the poor, of the	43
Synod, to priests assembled in a	121
Talent, against those who hide the LORD's	111
Teaching and example, that enormous sinners, when converted, may be profitable to others by their	68
Temperance, or sobriety, of..	36
—— and carnal desires, of	37
—— of	85
Temporal benefits, good works not to be done for, but for the sake of GOD	53
—— reward, that they deserve who labour in spiritual things	111
Tempt GOD, against those that	74
Temptation, of	74
Theft and thieves, against	38
Things, small, against those who neglect	59
Thomas, S.	122
Thought, of, which weighs cogitations	86
—— wandering of, and inconstancy, against	80
Thoughts, good, and meditations, of	91
—— evil, against	91
—— that GOD not only sees deeds but	88
Time, and its loss, of	59
Tithes, against those who keep back	38
Tongue, against a boasting..	61
—— against a contentious.	63
—— of the sins of the....	61
—— watchfulness over ..	64
—— against a, that seduces to sin	63

	PAGE
Transitory things, we must not trust in	40
Translation of Saints, the....	128
Tribulation, that it instructs..	76
—— that it increases and fertilizes	76
—— that it examines and purges	77
—— that it defends	77
—— that it crowns	77
—— that a man is known by	77
—— that GOD is often sought in	76
—— is to be embraced for the sake of GOD	75
Trinity, of the; and plurality of Persons	115
Trust in the LORD, that we must always	40
Truth, of	64
—— sometimes to be kept back	97
Tumults, of those that pacify	57
Understanding, that it is deservedly taken away from those who do evil works ..	00
Unfruitful, the, will be cut off	83
Union of mercy and justice, of the	44
Unity and concord, of, and their fruits	57
—— and eternity and power of GOD, of the	115
Usefulness of good companionship, of the	84
Vain dreams, against	58
Vain-glory, against	52
Vanity of man, of the	52
Vengeance and anger of GOD, of the	118
Venial sins and omissions, against	59
Vices, that we must cast out all	66
—— of the manifold setting forth of	66

INDEX.

	PAGE
Victory, temporal or spiritual, to be ascribed to GOD	79
Vincent, S.	122
Virgin, the Blessed, Nativity of	125
—— the festival of one	127
—— and Martyr, the festival of one	127
Virgins, the festival of many	128
Virtues, that he who would ascend to, must first descend by humility	50
—— of the manifold setting forth of	65
Visiting the poor, of	47
—— the sick, of	47
Vow or promise, against indiscreetly	62
Watchful, that we must be	58
—— against an evil security, because the day of the LORD will come like a thief	58
Watchfulness, of	83
—— over the tongue, of	64
Way of the LORD is narrow at the beginning, but in the end broad and pleasant	75
Weak things of the world, the LORD hath chosen	50
Weep abundantly, that we ought to for our sins	70
Well-doing, that the lives of the Saints are our incitements to	90
Whisperers and double-tongued men, against	62
Wicked, of the pusillanimity of the	88
—— superiors to be obeyed, if they command that which is consistent with GOD's will	52
—— the eyes of the will be opened after they are cast into hell	84
—— that they hate those who correct them	107
Wicked, the company of, sometimes to be tolerated	83
—— concerning the bitterness of the life of the	82
—— the, neither feel nor care for the labour which they undergo for the world	82
—— the, to be avoided	83
—— the bodies of, altogether polluted with sin	82
—— against the hope of the	40
—— that GOD's mysteries are not to be revealed or preached to the	111
—— ecclesiastics are worse than wicked laymen	104
Will of this world, against the	95
Wisdom, that we ought to take pleasure in seeking out and hearing	94
—— is to be sought, not only by reading and meditation, but by prayer and good works	94
—— the grace of, is not acquired by human virtue, but is given by GOD	94
—— that in solitude we have leisure for the study of	93
—— principally obtained by loving GOD	94
—— of the greatness of the consolation of Divine	95
—— of the benefit to be derived from the contemplation of	95
—— that there is none where sin reigns	95
—— of the continual meditation of	94
Wise, above that which is written, that we are not to be	99
Word, of the Eternal, and His eternal generation	115

L

Word of God, of hunger for the 112
—— must be obeyed, and not heard only 112
Words, that all our's should be to edification 63
—— of the LORD, against those who cut short 99
Works, we are not to seek the favour of man in our 53
—— against those that ascribe their's to their own strength 54
—— evil, that the understanding is deservedly taken away from those who do .. 90
—— good, of doing them with gladness 59
—— good, to be done for the sake of GOD, and not for temporal benefits 53
—— good, that we ought to hide our 54

Works, good, that the understanding of, is rightly given to those who are pure and humble.................. 89
—— of mercy, of the...... 47
World and sin, of conversion from the 67
—— against those who, through fear of this, do ill, or neglect to do well 108
—— against the will of this 95
—— that the wicked neither feel nor care for the labour which they undergo for the 82
—— of those who trample upon the 41
—— against the sorrows of this 58
Worldly knowledge, against too much attention to 96

Zeal of prelates, of the 105

Printed by J. SWIFT, Regent Press, 55, King-street, Regent-street.

WORKS
BY THE
LATE REV. DR. NEALE.

THE LAST TWO WORKS BY THE AUTHOR, ON HIS SICK BED.

ORIGINAL SEQUENCES, HYMNS, ETC. With
Prologue in "dear memory of JOHN KEBLE." 2s. 6d.; by post, 2s. 9d.

STABAT MATER SPECIOSA : FULL OF BEAUTY STOOD THE MOTHER. 1s.; by post, 1s. 2d.

A VOLUME OF SERMONS ON "THE SONG OF SONGS."
Edited by the Rev. J. HASKOLL, Rector of East Barkwith, Wragby. *Second Edition.* 5s.; by post, 5s. 4d.

THE PRIMITIVE LITURGIES, (IN GREEK,) OF S. MARK, S. CLEMENT, S. JAMES, S. CHRYSOSTOM, and S. BASIL.
Second Edition. With Preface by the Rev. Dr. LITTLEDALE. 6s.; by post, 6s. 2d.

THE TRANSLATIONS OF THE ABOVE PRIMITIVE LITURGIES.
With Introduction and Appendices. 4s.; by post, 4s. 3d.

HYMNS OF THE EASTERN CHURCH. TRANSLATED.
"They are literally, I believe, the *only* English versions of any part of the treasures of Oriental Hymnology."—*Preface.*

WORKS BY THE LATE DR. NEALE—(Continued.)

THE RHYTHM OF BERNARD OF MORLAIX, ON THE CELESTIAL COUNTRY.
TRANSLATED. On Toned Paper, cloth, 2s.; by post, 2s. 2d. In Calf, 7s. 6d.; by post, 7s. 9d. In Morocco, 8s. 6d.; by post, 8s. 9d.

The Cheap Edition, 8d.; by post, 9d.

Also, the Companion Volume to the "RHYTHM."

HYMNS ON THE JOYS AND GLORIES OF PARADISE.
1s. 6d.; by post, 1s. 7d.

HYMNS SUITABLE FOR INVALIDS.
On Toned Paper, 2s.; by post, 2s. 2d.

The Cheap Edition, 1s.; by post, 1s. 1d.

NOTES, ECCLESIOLOGICAL AND PICTURESQUE,
on DALMATIA, CROATIA, ISTRIA, and STYRIA, with a Visit to MONTENEGRO. 6s.; by post, 6s. 4d.

TEXT EMBLEMS: a Series of Twelve beautiful Designs, by DALZIEL, illustrative of the Mystical Interpretation of as many Verses from the Old Testament. 2s.; by post, 2s. 1d.

"THE CHRISTIAN NURSE;" AND HER MISSION IN THE SICK ROOM. Translated from the French of Father Gautrelet, by one of the Sisters of S. Margaret's, East Grinstead. 2s.; by post, 2s. 1d.

THE FARM OF APTONGA: a Story for Children of the Times of S. Cyprian. 1s.; by post, 1s. 2d. In Cloth, 2s.; by post, 2s. 2d.

Kept on Sale. (Printed at the Burntisland Press.)

THE ANCIENT LITURGIES OF THE GALLICAN CHURCH.
Now first Collected, with an Introductory Dissertation Notes, and various Readings, together with Parallel Passages from the Roman, Ambrosian, and Mozarabic Rites. Parts I. and II., 2s. 6d. each; by post, 2s. 8d.

J. T. HAYES, LYALL PLACE, EATON SQUARE, S.W.

www.ingramcontent.com/pod-product-compliance
Lightning Source LLC
Chambersburg PA
CBHW030347170426
43202CB00010B/1272